A Handrail for Healing:

Journaling Your Grief

Judith Feist

"A Handrail for Healing: Journaling Your Grief" copyright 2020 by Judith Feist.

All rights reserved. No part of this book may be reproduced in any form whatsoever, by photography or xerography or by any other means, by broadcast or transmission, by translation into any kind of language, nor by recording electronically or otherwise, without permission in writing from the author, except by a reviewer, who may quote brief passages in critical articles or reviews.

Edited by Alicia Ester
Interior illustration by Athena Currier
Photographs by Kurt Homan from the photo series Pandiculation (2005)

ISBN 13: 978-1-64343-878-8
Printed in the United States of America
First Printing: 2020
24 23 22 21 20   5 4 3 2 1

Cover and interior design by Dan Pitts

BEAVER'S POND PRESS

Beaver's Pond Press, Inc.
939 Seventh Street West
Saint Paul, Minnesota 55102
(952) 829-8818
www.BeaversPondPress.com

To Life.
It takes us places we do not want to go
and gives us chances to learn who we really are.

Introduction

It should come as no surprise that some of the people you love are going to die before you do. When they do, you will begin to tell yourself a story about your time with them and your coming time without them. How well you recover from feeling lost depends on this story. Is it ugly and angry? Is it a source of comfort and love? Is it filled with *what if*'s? Is it too short? Most likely it will be all of these things and more. And even if you never tell this story out loud to another soul, it will frame your future. This journal presents a way to think about your story with your loved ones and express your feelings about your life with and without them.

The sense of loss you feel after a death can level your life to bare ground, and you can grieve so deeply that getting up in the morning is a challenge. Thus begin the days of playing lost and found with your own life. You can feel like you do not belong anywhere, maybe for weeks, maybe for months, maybe for years.

My own journey into a life gone astray began with a divorce after thirty years of marriage. Counseling, walking, and music helped me work through those days. In 2002, I met Bob. After seven years of marriage, his death from mantel cell lymphoma in 2013 led me into the grief that still colors my life. The healing process has been complicated by two bouts of lymphoma of my own, which have required two rounds of chemotherapy, one in 2014 and the other in 2017, followed by two years of a maintenance protocol. I am told my life sounds like the plot of a Lifetime movie. That may be true, but I am living each day with more resolve to leave life with no regrets. This journal was one way for me to find solace in the truly dark places, and I hope it will light the path for you.

I offer you a peek into my journey as you work through the following questions, music cues, and observations that helped me. Give them a chance to alter your darkness as you perhaps doodle on the page, rage against your reality, or toss the book to the floor. There is no right or wrong response to grief. There are only feelings that you can honor by calling them out, listening to them, learning from them, and then letting them go. In the process, I hope you'll find a new reality to be faced with courage.

And perhaps writing your thoughts in this journal as you trudge your way through grief will not help. There are times when absolutely nothing does, not the wisest of observations, the warmest embrace, or the unwitting platitudes innocently offered. When the busy distractions are over, the ache remains. There are no dates in this book, because grief doesn't follow an exact timeline. If the journal isn't helping you now, put it aside for a time when you think it might.

We often frame the lives we are traveling through with metaphors that carry meaning for us. The two metaphors I use in this journal are stairs and the Slinky. We all know what stairs are, but if you are young, you might have never played with a Slinky toy. A Slinky is made up of continuous metal coils that stand tight when you set it upright, but when you put the coils on the top step of a staircase, open them, and let them go, they will walk down the stairs, and maybe move across the floor.

For this book and this journey, I want you to imagine you are sitting on a set of intimidating stairs. You likely see yourself on the bottom step, looking up in your grief and wondering how you can ever climb far enough to be healed. But I want you to imagine that you are sitting on the top step, just like the Slinky, and that your way through the loss is to push yourself off that top step, to let yourself fall, and to have faith that as you move from step to step you will find God's love and healing.

Along your day-to-day trip down the staircase you will find, if you open your heart to see, angels shining with God's love just for you. This love can make you angry at God, who will not love you only as you want. This God has gifts for you that you may not see or value as you mourn the way life used to be.

The final observation I have to offer here is a blessing and a curse that has been made by many others over the centuries: God has given your happiness directly to you and not to any other humans, events, or situations. That means that your spouse, children, friends, family, job, success, failure, or the condition of your living room floor do not control how happy you are as a person.

It is a blessing because you get to be happy if you choose to be; it is a curse because you have no one to blame if you are not happy. The loss of a loved one is a huge challenge to this blessing, a challenge that you, and I, will face every day for the rest of our lives. I pray that you will face it with the courage to live simply by offering God's love to those life brings your way.

Now, what is the story you are telling yourself about how the rest of your life going to be?

How to Use This Journal

ABOUT THE SONGS

The songs that begin each daily prompt express some aspect of life and loss. They come from all genres of music, and some are purely instrumental. They are all available to listen to on YouTube or other music streaming sources. You may like some of them and dislike others, but music is a universal language that can help heal the pain in the human heart. You have nothing to lose by giving them a try. If certain songs don't work, try finding others that do. Or look for other artists who sing the same song; you may like their versions better. The blank pages at the end of the journal are ready for you to create your own grief song lists.

ABOUT THE OBSERVATIONS

These observations about life and grief come from everywhere wisdom enters the world. The ideas are certainly not new, but maybe they will be new to you. My hope is that they will help you think about how you are feeling.

ABOUT YOUR RESPONSE

All of these prompts are places I have found myself in the last six years of grief. And if I let myself, I can still hear what my answers would be as I managed my denial, anger, broken heart, memories, acceptance, and attempts at moving on. I hope you will impulsively write down the first thing you say to yourself without censoring what comes. There is no wrong or right answer, only what lives in your experience and feels true for you. If you don't find words, feel free to draw or respond in another way.

WORKING AND WALKING

When nothing helps with the grieving process, there are two final things to try.

The first is walking out the front door. Even five minutes a day of walking can give you a sense of control, as in *I can do this one thing*. Taking music along to make the walk longer is an enhancement. The goal is to become a person who moves, a Walkologist, an expert in exercise for your own life.

The second is working. There is something in your life that needs to be done: go and do it. Work with what is in your hands right now. Then as you move forward, find either an old job from your past that you had given up and return to it, or a new job that suits your future in some way not apparent until now. The goal is to become a person who is useful, a Workologist, an expert in the work you are called to do in your own life.

*So begin at whatever spot
in the journal you choose,
date the page, and let the
music and the message speak to you.
Then find your voice and respond.*

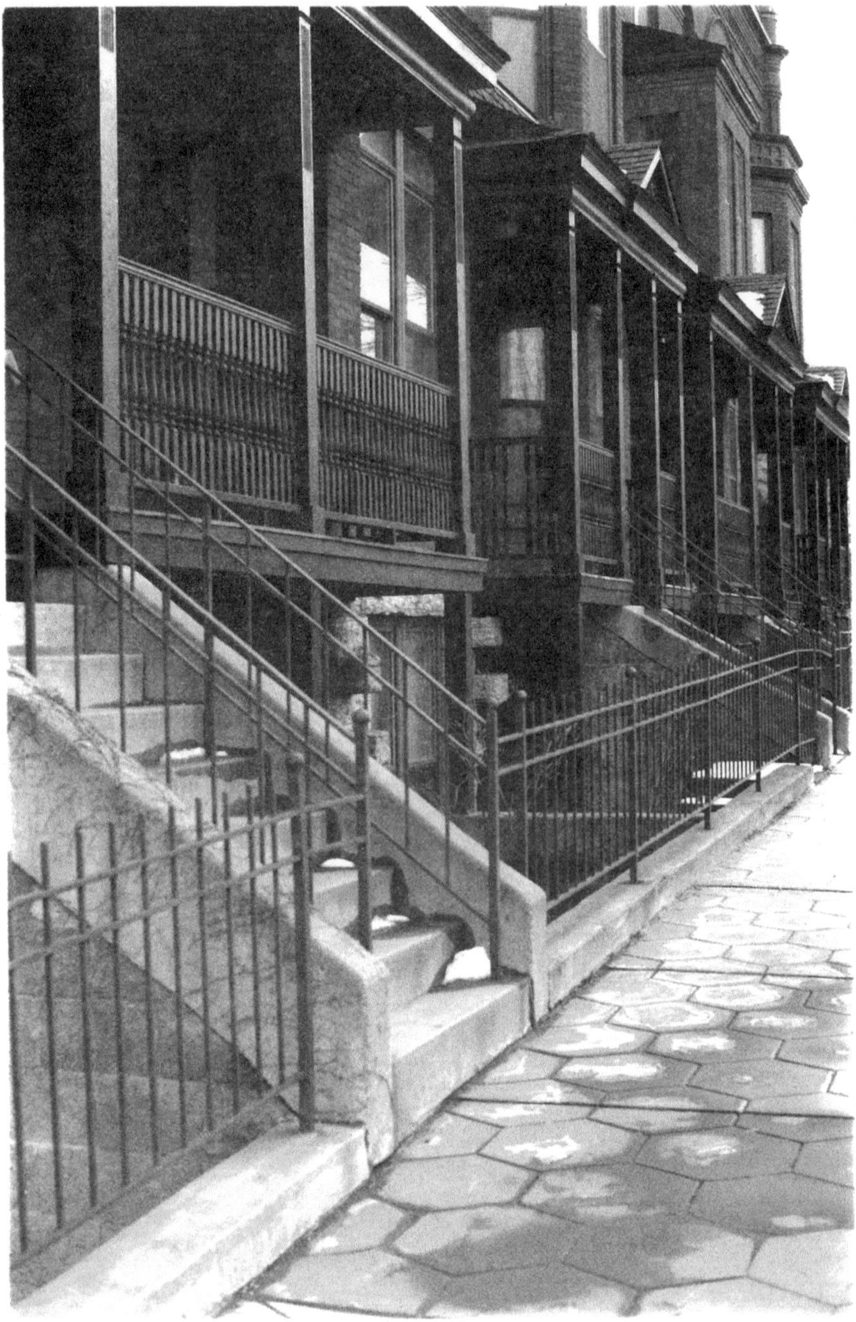

Two Years in September

The days race away
From the day you left me.

Cascading down
Into the hole,
The emptiness I
Try to live with.

They drag me along
Barely hanging on, screaming
Stop, please, stop.
Stop the world from moving on.

How that would help
I do not know.
But then, nothing helps.

The ache is
Massive, endless;
Slowly drowning what is
Left of me.

So time heals all wounds.
Sure!
Fucking when?

It will be two years
In September.

DENIAL   Date_____

Song: "Music Fills the Spaces" The Sweet Remains

Observation: From a certain perspective, nothing ever dies.

Your Response: Why should I . . . . .

ANGER   Date_____

Song: "It Goes On and On" The Avett Brothers

Observation: You have to show up in your own life.

Your Response: I don't care if . . . . .

BROKEN HEART   Date_____

Song: "If I Could" Jack Johnson

Observation: Cry for your right to a new love.

Your Response: How could you . . . . .

REMEMBERING   Date_____

Song: "Come Healing" Leonard Cohen

Just what you wanted to hear: God never gives you more than you can handle.

Your Response: Don't tell me to . . . . .

ACCEPTANCE   Date_____

Song: "I Can Let Go Now" Alison Krauss & Union Station

Observation: The world demands that you move fast; the infinite demands the slowness of time.

Your Response: I did not know . . . . .

MOVING ON   Date_____

Song: "A Matter of Trust" Billy Joel

Observation: Blessing or curse: there are no do-overs with death?

Your Response: God owes me . . . . .

DENIAL   Date_____

Song: "Is There a God?" Jack Broadbent

Observation: Love is any act of willful acceptance of others and life.

Your Response: I should have told you . . . . .

ANGER   Date_____

Song: "Anthem" Leonard Cohen

Observation: Is living in anger, doubt, and fear the human default position?

Your Response: The whole world can . . . . .

BROKEN HEART   Date_____

Song: "Must Be Something I Missed" Kenny Chesney

Observation: Tears can be the presence of what seems like endless brokenness.

Your Response: Please make it . . . . .

REMEMBERING   Date_____

Song: "I Want You" Morgan James

Observation: Joy is our response to learning how to just be grateful.

Your Response: It is so hard to . . . . .

ACCEPTANCE   Date_____

Song: "More Than One Way Home" Keb' Mo'

Observation: Wash the dishes, go to work, take care of your family. This is how you find peace.

Your Response: The truth is . . . . .

MOVING ON   Date_____

Song: "Home" Joyann Parker

Observation: Find how to love today, especially when you'd rather not.

Your Response: I will never . . . . .

DENIAL   Date_____

Song: "I'm So Tired" The Beatles

Observation: Life does not come with a timely warning of what is ahead.

Your Response: I hate . . . . .

ANGER   Date_____

Song: "Gravedigger" Dave Matthews

Observation: You have nothing to prove to God, only to yourself.

Your Response: I will never . . . . .

BROKEN HEART   Date_____

Song: "I Am a Man of Constant Sorrow" The Soggy Bottom Boys

Observation: When things seem so wrong, say to yourself, "I do not know what this means."

Your Response: Give me back . . . . .

REMEMBERING   Date_____

Song: "Cry Like a Rainstorm" Bonnie Raitt

Observation: Now you need a new purpose for your life. Find the one sent from God.

Your Response: Will anyone ever . . . . .

ACCEPTANCE   Date_____

Song: "Learned A Lot" Amos Lee

Observation: Love is like gravity holding the universe together. Love holds us together.

Your Response: My life is . . . . .

MOVING ON   Date_____

Song: "Athair Are Neamh" Enya

Observation: When you bring the best ingredients to your own life, you can let go of the consequences.

Your Response: God owes me . . . . .

DENIAL   Date_____

Song: "Ghost of Myself" The Steel Wheels

Observation: Some events will always feel like they just happened yesterday.

Your Response: I do not believe . . . . .

ANGER   Date_____

Song: "Buckets of Rain" Bob Dylan

Observation: Confession is agreeing with what God says is true of your life.

Your Response: I was wrong . . . . .

BROKEN HEART   Date_____

Song: "Wolves" Garth Brooks

Observation: What you don't know can beat the life out of you.

Your Response: Why should I . . . . .

REMEMBERING   Date_____

Song: "Whenever I Say Your Name" Sting featuring Mary J. Blige

Observation: When fear shows up at your table, don't invite it to dine.

Your Response: If only . . . . .

ACCEPTANCE   Date_____

Song: "One Thing I Know" Selah

Observation: To find the light in your life you have to move forward.

Your Response: It makes me so angry . . . . .

MOVING ON   Date_____

Song: "I Came Here to Live" Trace Adkins

Observation: The only thing I have to give is what is in my heart. Let's hope peace lives there.

Your Response: It is so hard to . . . . .

## DENIAL	Date_____

Song: "When Love Is Gone" The Muppet Christmas Carol

Observation: There can be more room for love in a broken heart.

Your Response: Time is . . . . .

## ANGER	Date_____

Song: "The Bug" Mary Chapin Carpenter

Observation: No one is ever truly ready to bounce off the merry-go-round that is life.

Your Response: It makes me so angry that . . . . .

BROKEN HEART   Date_____

Song: "Forever Autumn" The Moody Blues

Observation: The truth can heal, but it often has to hurt first.

Your Response: The world is . . . . .

REMEMBERING   Date_____

Song: "Beauty in the Word" Macy Gray

Observation: Know what is true in your own life, and speak it.

Your Response: My heart . . . . .

ACCEPTANCE   Date_____

Song: "Round and Round" Kenny Chesney

Observation: The goal is not to let go of the dead; it is to let them shine through you.

Your Response: I want . . . . .

MOVING ON   Date_____

Song: "Forever Young" Bob Dylan

Observation: When we exercise intensely, we will hit the wall but keep going. Surviving grief is just like that. We must keep going.

Your Response: God is . . . . .

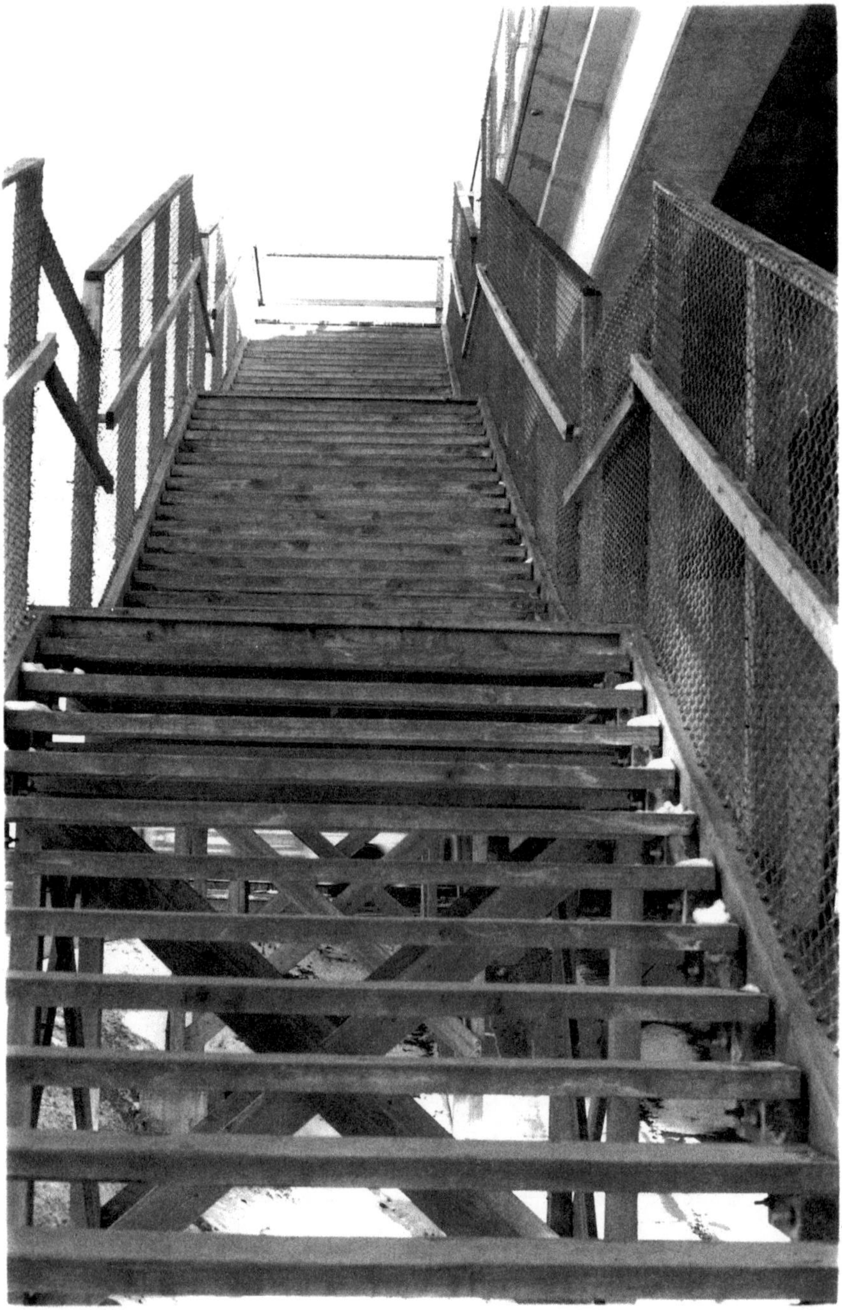

Carrying My Dead

I cannot write what
I do not know
And I do not know how
To carry my dead.
I do not even know
If I should be
Carrying my dead.

Perhaps I was supposed
To leave him somewhere
Along the road during
The last two years
since he left me.

But he will not stay gone.
His leaving colors my
Every breath with a sadness
That will not let go of me.

So how do I live and
carry my dead?

How do I birth the
New me who is able to smile
And look forward to
A new day?

Or are tears and longing
All that are left of this
Thing we call life?

DENIAL   Date_____

Song: "Sad Songs (Say So Much)" Elton John

Observation: If death were final, the spirit of joy would vanish from the earth.

Your Response: If only . . . . .

ANGER   Date_____

Song: "Take Another Road" Jimmy Buffett

Observation: I do not like the game of lost and found loves.

Your Response: The world is . . . . .

BROKEN HEART   Date_____

Song: "Angel" John Proulx

Observation: Life is possible because death creates the soil for renewal.

Your Response: My days are so . . . . .

REMEMBERING   Date_____

Song: "If I Didn't Know Any Better" Alison Krauss & Union Station

Observation: The Ojibwa embrace the gifts of the seven grandfathers, knowledge for their community. Can you embrace Minwaadendamowin (respect)?

Your Response: Will anyone ever . . . . .

ACCEPTANCE   Date_____

Song: "That's Life" Frank Sinatra

Observation: Impermanence is a gift. Imagine if nothing ever changed.

Your Response: I want . . . . .

MOVING ON   Date_____

Song: "The Perfect Kiss" Bette Midler

Observation: Only in the movies does the music hint at what might be coming.

Your Response: I hate . . . . .

DENIAL   Date_____

Song: "Demons" Imagine Dragons

Observation: I want no part of the easy road; it leads to more pain, not less.

Your Response: God is . . . . .

ANGER   Date_____

Song: "Because You Loved Me" Celine Dion

Observation: Ego at its most deceptive says I am not good enough for myself or you, much less for God.

Your Response: The world is . . . . .

BROKEN HEART   Date_____

Song: "Radio" The Corrs

Observation: Life is fair. Each one of us is unique; we get to choose how to live, and we all die. But what happens along the way can exhaust your heart.

Your Response: My life is so . . . . .

REMEMBERING   Date_____

Song: "Sideways" Citizen Cope

Observation: Real gratitude cannot be taught, but perhaps it can be caught.

Your Response: Show me . . . . .

ACCEPTANCE   Date_____

Song: "My Peace" Arlo Guthrie

Observation: Life is endless possibilities, eternal uncertainty, with each moment creating the next.

Your Response: I do not believe . . . . .

MOVING ON   Date_____

Song: "I Think It's Going to Rain Today" Nina Simone

Observation: It is very difficult to sit in silence, waiting for what's next in your life.

Your Response: Why should I . . . . .

DENIAL   Date_____

Song: "Island" Eddy Raven

Observation: Denial is the stage of life where we don't trust God for our lives.

Your Response: If only . . . . .

ANGER   Date_____

Song: "If God Will Send His Angels" U2

Observation: Is anger the black hole you have fallen into?

Your Response: I will never . . . . .

BROKEN HEART   Date_____

Song: "I Know You're Out There Somewhere" The Moody Blues

Observation: Hope is a weapon we use against ourselves.

Your Response: Just tell me . . . . .

REMEMBERING   Date_____

Song: "All Alright" Zac Brown Band

Just what you wanted to hear: This too shall pass.

Your Response: Time is . . . . .

ACCEPTANCE   Date_____

Song: "Give Them Love" Mishka

Observation: Life is in the child we take care of, the sudden insight we receive, the unexpected act of kindness we experience.

Your Response: I am sorry . . . . .

MOVING ON   Date_____

Song: "A Lot of Things Different" Kenny Chesney

Observation: Lay your desires at God's feet. If they belong to you, God will give them back to you.

Your Response: I hate . . . . .

DENIAL   Date_____

Song: "Life Is Better With You" Michael Franti & Spearhead

Observation: Being confused is a grace from God. Don't hold on tightly to what you think you want.

Your Response: It makes me so angry that . . . . .

ANGER   Date_____

Song: "Purple Rain" Prince

Observation: Lay anger down at God's feet. It is far too toxic to carry.

Your Response: I don't care if . . . . .

BROKEN HEART   Date_____

Song: "Boats" Kenny Chesney

Observation: A broken heart can make more room for growth.

Your Response: Help me . . . . .

REMEMBERING   Date_____

Song: "Immortality" Celine Dion featuring the Bee Gees

Observation: Love reaches out endlessly. There is no way it can spend all of its self.

Your Response: My heart is . . . . .

ACCEPTANCE   Date_____

Song: "My Poor Old Heart" Alison Krauss & Union Station

Observation: Freedom is the definition of love: you set free those you love.

Your Response: I should have told you . . . . .

MOVING ON   Date_____

Song: "Spirit" Al Jarreau

Observation: What is mine will come to me when I need it and stay until the need is fulfilled.

Your Response: Show me . . . . .

DENIAL   Date_____

Song: "Good Day to Cry" Beth Hart

Observation: In loving me, you put value to my life. It is a currency I do not know how to spend.

Your Response: Don't tell me . . . . .

ANGER   Date_____

Song: "A Change Would Do You Good" Sheryl Crow

Observation: Anger is the soul's voice asking us to choose love over fear.

Your Response: Give me back . . . . .

BROKEN HEART   Date_____

Song: "Carry On" Pat Green

Observation: Faith and utter confusion always live in the same heart.

Your Response: Please make it . . . . .

REMEMBERING   Date_____

Song: "Here Comes That Rainbow Again" Kris Kristofferson

Observation: God does not change so we can.

Your Response: I was wrong . . . . .

ACCEPTANCE   Date_____

Song: "So Good" Al Jarreau

Observation: Maybe all that can be found in earthly mysteries is trust.

Your Response: I do not believe . . . . .

MOVING ON   Date_____

Song: "Get Back on That Pony" Chris LeDoux

Observation: It is hard to move on when you feel befucked by your own life.

Your Response: I did not know . . . . .

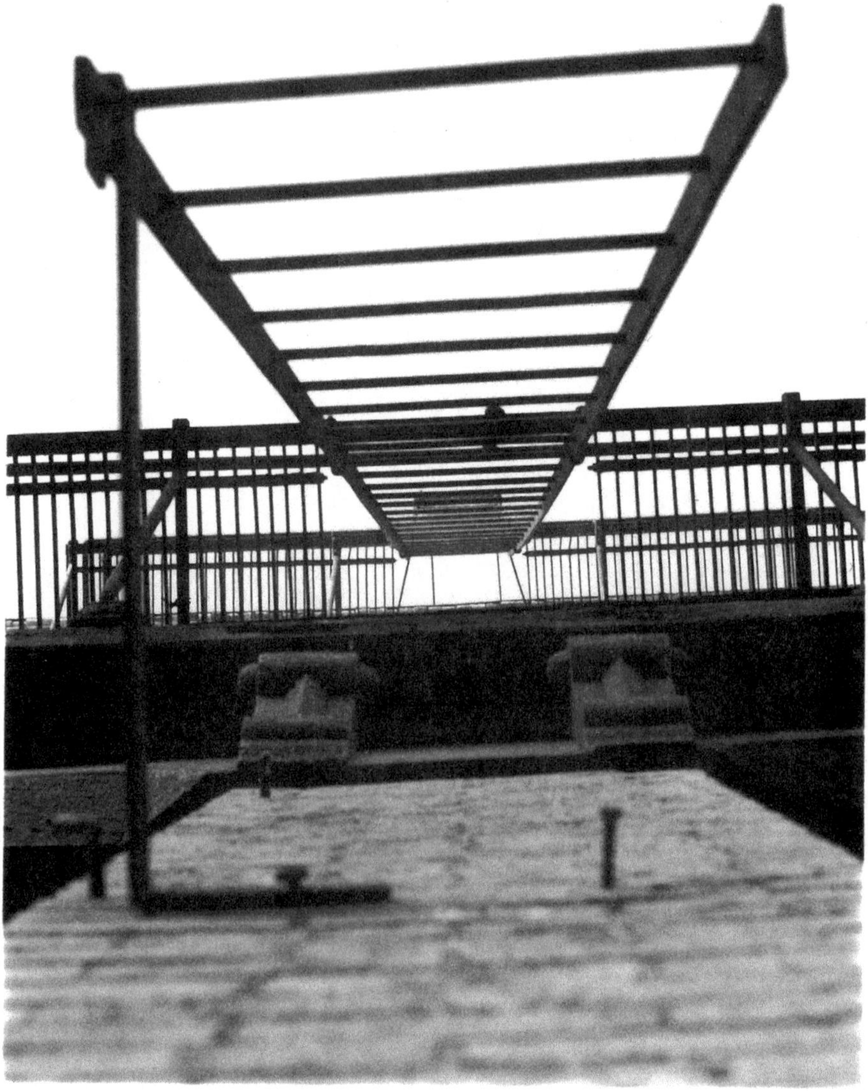

Did You Know

Did you know all
Love went with you
when you died?

Now I can find only need.

The need to hold your hand.

The need to walk with you.

The need to see your smile.

The need to hear you laugh.

The need to wake with you
By my side.

The need to wrap myself
In your physical presence.

Someday,
Will the love
Come back to me in
Memories sweetened
By a life reborn
Free from need?

DENIAL   Date_____

Song: "1942, From Russia" Keiko Matsui

Observation: A greeting card can only hint at God's mercy.

Your Response: I was wrong . . . . .

ANGER   Date_____

Song: "In the End" Kelley Hunt

Just what you wanted to hear: Why can't you be more like . . . ?

Your Response: Help me . . . . .

BROKEN HEART   Date_____

Song: "It Only Hurts When I Cry" Dwight Yoakam

Observation: What if I never have anything in my hands again that is truly mine?

Your Response: God has . . . . .

REMEMBERING   Date_____

Song: "My One and Only Love" Chris Botti and Paula Cole

Observation: The Ojibwa embrace the gifts of the seven grandfathers. Can you embrace Miigwe'aadiziwin (generosity)?

Your Response: Give me back . . . . .

ACCEPTANCE   Date_____

Song: "Sunday Mornin' Comin' Down" Kris Kristofferson

Observation: I still have bad days, but that's okay. I used to have bad years.

Your Response: Just tell me . . . . .

MOVING ON   Date_____

Song: "Off to See the Lizard" Jimmy Buffett

Observation: Would it feel better if you could punish someone for your loss?

Your Response: I'm sorry . . . . .

DENIAL   Date_____

Song: "Hearts Have Turned to Stone" Elton John and Leon Russell

Observation: Like a joyous toddler, God colors outside of my lines.

Your Response: God is . . . . .

ANGER   Date_____

Song: "Spirit of a Storm" Kenny Chesney

Observation: Victory belongs to the patient ever-opening flower.

Your Response: Just tell me . . . . .

BROKEN HEART   Date_____

Song: "You Are My Sunshine" Jamey Johnson, Twiggy Ramirez, and Shooter Jennings

Observation: What shines through the cracks of your broken heart, love or fear?

Your Response: Show me . . . . .

REMEMBERING   Date_____

Song: "Miss Emily's Picture" John Conlee

Observation: Memory is a choice; what do you choose to remember?

Your Response: It makes me so angry that . . . . .

ACCEPTANCE   Date_____

Song: "For the Good Times" Kris Kristofferson

Observation: Tomorrow's abundance is created by today's acts of kindness and generosity.

Your Response: If only . . . . .

MOVING ON   Date_____

Song: "Brick by Brick" Kelley Hunt

Observation: Give love to yourself so that you do not demand it from others.

Your Response: I should have told you . . . . .

DENIAL   Date_____

Song: "No Love Today" Chris Smither

Observation: Our story is either a curse or a cure.

Your Response: My heart won't . . . . .

ANGER   Date_____

Song: "Moon on My Shoulder" Lyle Lovett

Observation: Being patient while you suffer creates space and time to grow.

Your Response: Don't tell me . . . . .

BROKEN HEART   Date_____

Song: "Only Love Can Break Your Heart" Neil Young

Observation: Hell is when you see no hope for anything new in your life.

Your Response: I did not know . . . . .

REMEMBERING   Date_____

Song: "It's Your Song" Garth Brooks

Observation: They say, "It is what it is." But it will also be what my mind makes of it.

Your Response: I will never . . . . .

ACCEPTANCE   Date_____

Song: "Grateful Moon" Sarah Morris

Observation: "More prisons are made of fear and guilt than stone." —Thich Nhat Hanh

Your Response: Time is . . . . .

MOVING ON   Date_____

Song: "Wear Your Love Like Heaven" Sarah McLachlan

Observation: Why is the word God gave me for my life the one I dislike the most? Who really wants to be patient?

Your Response: Help me . . . . .

DENIAL   Date_____

Song: "Sometimes I Feel Like a Motherless Child" Jimmy Scott

Observation: What is the pain you will not let go of?

Your Observation: Why should I . . . . .

ANGER   Date_____

Song: "Nothin'" Robert Plant & Alison Krauss

Observation: Did you find the bread crumbs of today's love hidden in the mundane stuff of life?

Your Response: It is so hard to . . . . .

BROKEN HEART   Date_____

Song: "When Am I Gonna Get Over You" LeAnn Rimes

Observation: The best prayers are those you do not understand.

Your Response: I was wrong . . . . .

REMEMBERING   Date_____

Song: "Accentuate the Positive" Dr. John

Observation: I am so hopelessly confused that God must be in control.

Your Response: I want . . . . .

ACCEPTANCE   Date_____

Song: "Bless the Broken Road" Rascal Flatts

Observation: Resolve to touch lives with the grace of an ordinary life.

Your Response: My life is . . . . .

MOVING ON   Date_____

Song: "Rocking Chair" Eric Clapton

Observation: Become the person you needed when you were younger.

Your Response: The truth is . . . . .

DENIAL   Date_____

Song: "Heaven Can Wait" Meat Loaf

Observation: You have to move slowly to keep up with God.

Your Response: Please make it . . . . .

ANGER   Date_____

Song: "Let It Rain" Eric Clapton

Observation: We all look away from death.

Your Response: Will anyone ever . . . . .

BROKEN HEART   Date_____

Song: "If My Heart Had Wings" Melissa Manchester

Observation: Brokenness is a gift of grace. The unbroken do not feel for the rest of the world.

Your Response: It makes me so angry that . . . . .

REMEMBERING   Date_____

Song: "On and On" Stephen Bishop

Observation: If you cannot set them free, you cannot call it love.

Your Response: The whole world can . . . . .

ACCEPTANCE   Date_____

Song: "Passera" Il Divo

Observation: You are not alive in either yesterday or tomorrow. But you are alive today; surrender to now.

Your Response: My heart . . . . .

MOVING ON   Date_____

Song: "Fragile" Sting

Observation: Death is a place in life that hurts, no matter what you do.

Your Response: How could you . . . . .

"Welcome to Heaven's Gate. Your call is very important to us. Please stay on the line and your call will be answered in the order received."

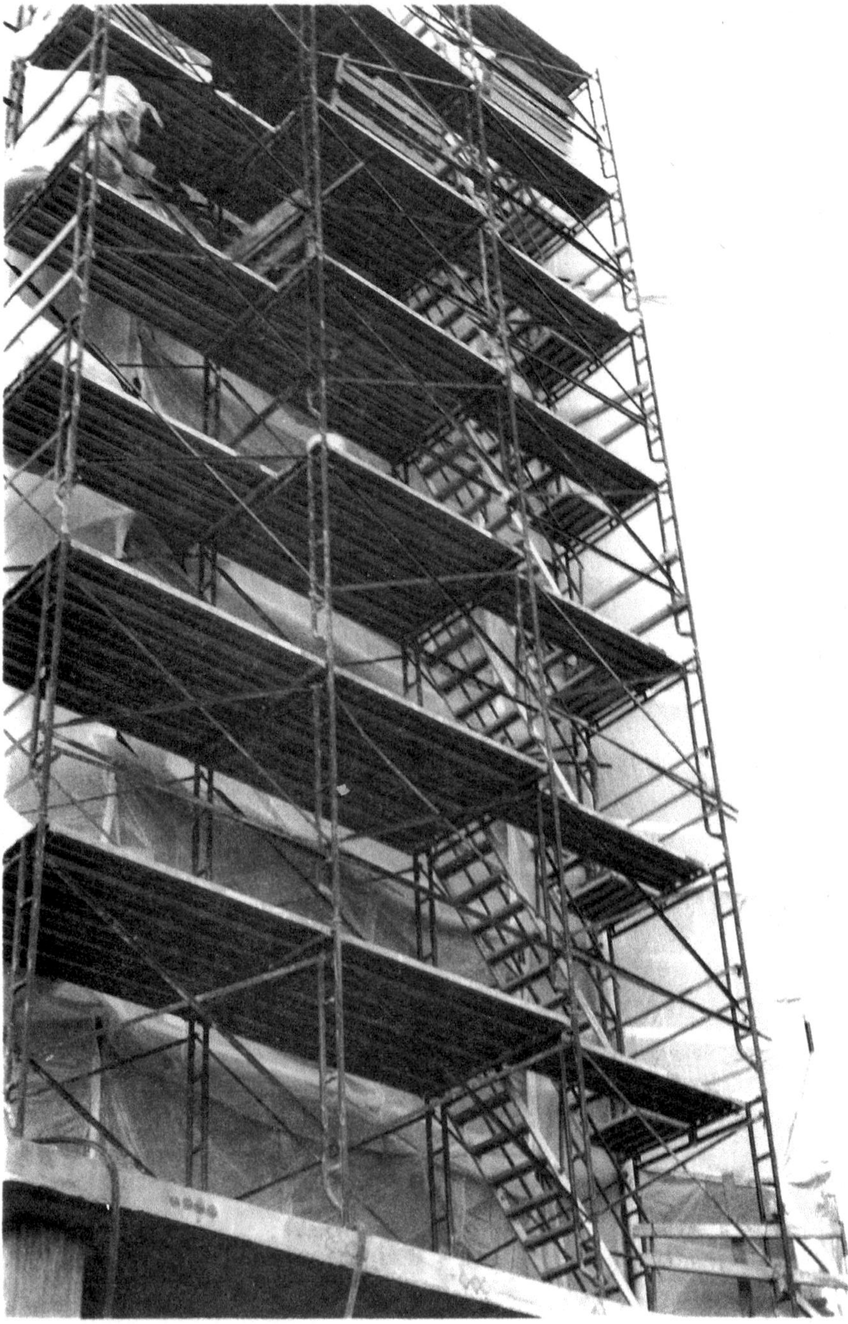

Sweet Water

How much pain
Lives inside
The woman who
Filters life into
Sweet water?

When dreams die
And life moves sideways
When breathing is more
Loss than love
And sadness oozes
Over my soul

Then I walk
Blindly into each day
With faith
Too small to find any
Joy in death.

Tears flow over
mud-covered knees
And trust is buried
So deep it cannot
light the way to
Anywhere.

Sweet water
Is an endless lake
Misting the air
As it tumbles
Down the mountain
Where my rutted
Path ends.

DENIAL   Date_____

Song: "I and Love and You" The Avett Brothers

Observation: Do you have the courage that lets God create your days?

Your Response: I did not know . . . . .

ANGER   Date_____

Song: "Tell Your Heart to Beat Again" Danny Gokey

Observation: Death is the black cloud in both your head and heart. It changes everything.

Your Response: It is so hard to . . . . .

BROKEN HEART   Date_____

Song: "Missing Your Love" Jonny Lang

Observation: Have no patience when your fear wears the mask of grief. Call it out.

Your Response: I was wrong . . . . .

REMEMBERING   Date_____

Song: "The Very Thought of You" Aaron Neville featuring Linda Ronstadt

Observation: The Ojibwa embrace the gifts of the seven grandfathers. Can you embrace Dibaadeniziwin (humility)?

Your Response: The truth is . . . . .

ACCEPTANCE   Date_____

Song: "Heart Full of Soul" Chris Isaak

Observation: Try to accept but not give in. Death and lost love come to everyone.

Your Response: My life is . . . . .

MOVING ON   Date_____

Song: "Roof Garden" Al Jarreau

Observation: Is a time of being alone required of you?

Your Response: I want . . . . .

DENIAL   Date_____

Song: "Will the Circle Be Unbroken" Nitty Gritty Dirt Band

Observation: Be calm when you face God.

Your Response: I love . . . . .

ANGER   Date_____

Song: "The Story So Far" Flogging Molly

Observation: Nothing is more dangerous to your ego than answered prayer.

Your Response: Show me . . . . .

BROKEN HEART   Date_____

Song: "Killing the Blues" Robert Plant & Alison Krauss

Observation: Real faith in God is born in the dark of the night.

Your Response: I was wrong . . . . .

REMEMBERING   Date_____

Song: "Heavy Cloud No Rain" Sting

Observation: The dream God has for you is more important than the dream you have for yourself.

Your Response: The truth is . . . . .

ACCEPTANCE   Date_____

Song: "Running on Faith" Eric Clapton

Observation: In order to be alive, illusions must die. What illusion of yours must die?

Your Response: My heart . . . . .

MOVING ON   Date_____

Song: "If I Ever Leave This World Alive" Flogging Molly

Observation: Do not despair the smallness of every beginning.

Your Response: I don't care if . . . . .

DENIAL   Date_____

Song: "Brand New Day" Sting

Observation: God did not cause this storm, but God can bring you through it.

Your Response: If only . . . . .

ANGER   Date_____

Song: "Pushing up Daisies" Garth Brooks

Observation: The chaos of your life is not punishment; it is a chance to choose a new way.

Your Response: How could you . . . . .

BROKEN HEART   Date_____

Song: "Grandma's Hands" Bill Withers

Observation: Love is the river that carries my heart home.

Your Response: Give me back my . . . . .

REMEMBERING   Date_____

Song: "Forever Love" Reba McEntire

Observation: The truth has both thorns and kindness.

Your Response: I should have told you . . . . .

ACCEPTANCE   Date_____

Song: "Uncloudy Day" Willie Nelson

Observation: A life can be right and still feel wrong.

Your Response: I do not believe . . . . .

MOVING ON   Date_____

Song: "Lean on Me" Bill Withers

Observation: The future lies in a passion for patience.

Your Response: I hate . . . . .

DENIAL   Date_____

Song: "I Don't Hurt Anymore" Martina McBride

Observation: The music of the eternal does not bend to the noise of earthly moments.

Your Response: Just tell me . . . . .

ANGER   Date_____

Song: "Make It Rain" Ed Sheeran

Just what you wanted to hear: I know exactly what you are feeling.

Your Response: Please make it . . . . .

BROKEN HEART   Date_____

Song: "And So It Goes" Billy Joel

Observation: There is no door, but keep on knocking.

Your Response: The whole world can . . . . .

REMEMBERING   Date_____

Song: "The Ballad of the Snow Leopard and the Tanqueray Cowboy" Lyle Lovett

Observation: I look for myself reflected in your eyes.

Your Response: My life is . . . . .

ACCEPTANCE   Date_____

Song: "Snowbird" Anne Murray

Observation: It is hard to escape the darkness when ordinary life has taken the light out of your world.

Your Response: Why should I . . . . .

MOVING ON   Date_____

Song: "'Til I Get It Right" Shawn Colvin

Observation: The right seemingly useless gesture makes a positive difference in this world.

Your Response: Give me back . . . . .

DENIAL   Date_____

Song: "Song for Life" Alison Krauss

Observation: Learn to find and trust the blessings of today.

Your Response: It makes me so angry that . . . . .

ANGER   Date_____

Song: "Hurt" Johnny Cash

Observation: Are my best jokes really behind me?

Your Response: Will anyone ever . . . . .

BROKEN HEART   Date_____

Song: "A Better Place" Glen Campbell

Observation: I have all that I need to live a godly life.

Your Response: Life owes me . . . . .

REMEMBERING   Date_____

Song: "That Old Glass Case" Paulette Carlson

Observation: What is the happy lie you told yourself?

Your Response: I love . . . . .

ACCEPTANCE   Date_____

Song: "Hallelujah" Susan Boyle

Observation: You need to choose God above all else; that is the hard truth about life.

Your Response: Just tell me . . . . .

MOVING ON   Date_____

Song: "Better When I'm Dancin'" Meghan Trainor

Observation: I need to find something that will balance what I have lost.

Your Response: Life owes me . . . . .

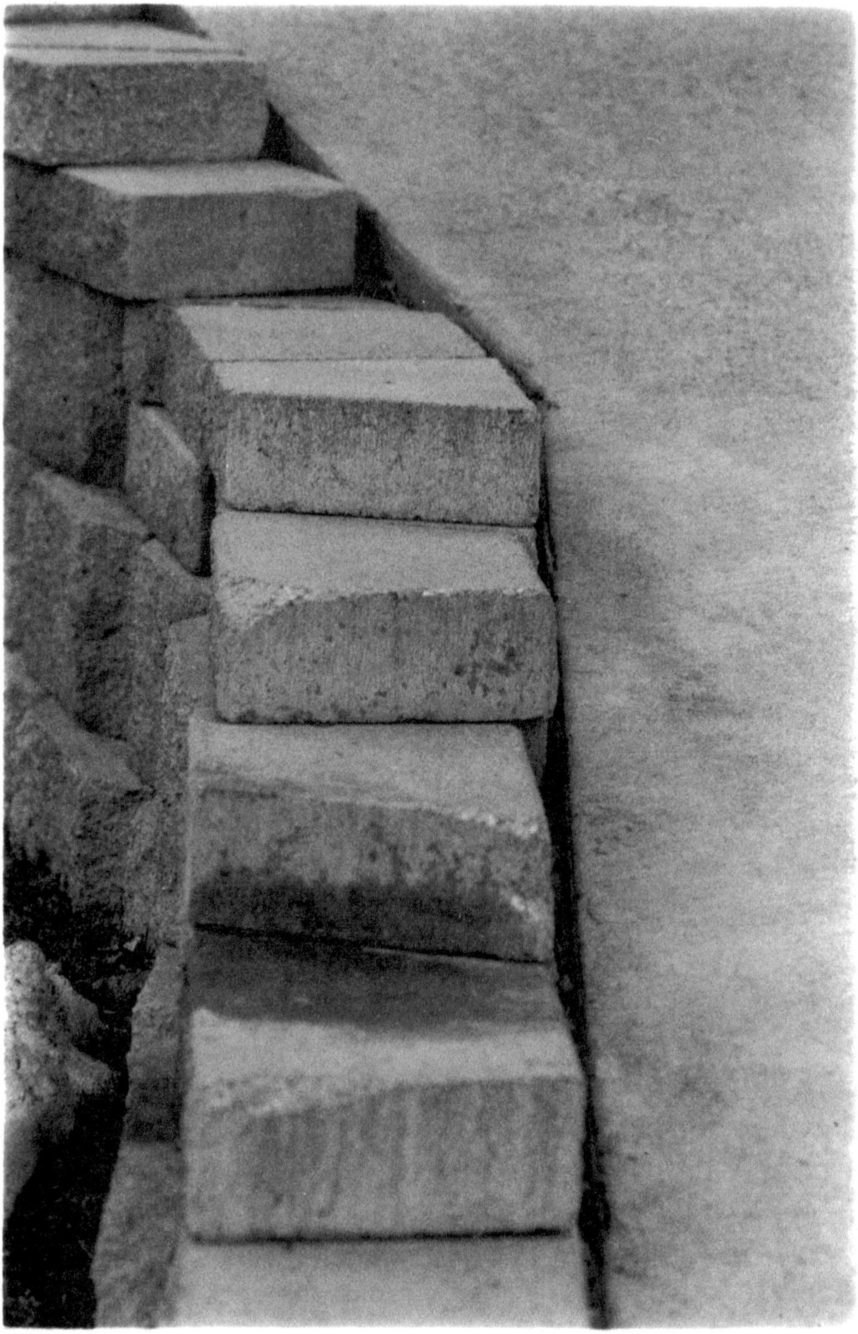

Death Has Come Knocking

Death has come knocking on my door.
It has stolen away the one I love,
The one that all my love did not save.

And all I want to do is dig
In the rocky ground,
Grind dirt under my fingernails,
Hack off dead branches, uproot weeds, break stones.

Please do not ask me to save the world.
For I could not save even the one I loved.

Ask me only to help grow
What will surely thrive
Without my tender care.
For that is without result.

Let me care only for that which I cannot kill.

DENIAL   Date_____

Song: "Waiting to Be Found" Susan Ashton

Observation: There is little joy in tomorrow if you don't see the angels of today.

Your Response: Just tell me . . . . .

ANGER   Date_____

Song: "I Cry Everyday" Shelby Lynne

Observation: Anger with a loss seems greater than happiness with a win.

Your Response: My days are so . . . . .

BROKEN HEART   Date_____

Song: "I Wonder" Chris Isaak

Observation: You can die from a broken heart, but would you want to?

Your Response: Show me . . . . .

REMEMBERING   Date_____

Song: "Remember" Harry Nilsson

Just what you wanted to hear: Time heals all wounds.

Your Response: The world is . . . . .

## ACCEPTANCE		Date_____

Song: "Light of a Clear Blue Morning" The Wailin' Jennys

Observation: Acceptance is the path through depression, which is not the same as conceding the journey to death.

Your Response: It makes me so angry that . . . . .

## MOVING ON		Date_____

Song: "I Shall Sing" Art Garfunkel

Observation: Your destiny lives in accepting the gift that has been placed in your hand.

Your Response: God is . . . . .

DENIAL   Date_____

Song: "Living the Blues" Tracy Nelson

Observation: Humans are the strongest, most fragile species on the planet.

Your Response: Give me back . . . . .

ANGER   Date_____

Song: "Nothing Without You" Bebo Norman

Observation: Death proves that we do not own the next minute, or today, much less tomorrow.

Your Response: Help me . . . . .

BROKEN HEART   Date_____

Song: "What Becomes of the Brokenhearted" Martina McBride

Observation: If life is for bringing the lost back to God, why does it feel like I am standing still?

Your Response: Show me . . . . .

REMEMBERING   Date_____

Song: "Why Oh Why" Celine Dion

Observation: God whispered to Adam and Eve as they walked out of the Garden of Eden, "Live Me the difference between life and death."

Your Response: Give me back . . . . .

ACCEPTANCE   Date_____

Song: "Cool Down" Mishka

Observation: Peace is so certain of God's love that it does not strive to change anything.

Your Response: I should have told you . . . . .

MOVING ON   Date_____

Song: "Before My Time" John Conlee

Observation: The new happiness feels like a betrayal of the life I had with you.

Your Observation: Don't tell me . . . . .

## DENIAL			Date_____

Song: "Stayin' Alive" Bee Gees

Observation: If your heart is open, God's angels will find you in your darkness.

Your Response: My days are so . . . . .

## ANGER			Date_____

Song: "Heaven's Only Days Down the Road" Shelby Lynne

Observation: My living room window is still intact because I cannot find a brick when I want one.

Your Response: I love . . . . .

BROKEN HEART   Date_____

Song: "Perfect Love . . . Gone Wrong" Sting

Observation: Time heals all wounds only when you use time to find new joyful experiences.

Your Response: Please make it . . . . .

REMEMBERING   Date_____

Song: "After the Rain Has Fallen" Sting

Observation: Life plows the same ground, endlessly, until we learn gratitude for who we are.

Your Response: The truth is . . . . .

ACCEPTANCE Date_____

Song: "If Tomorrow Never Comes" Garth Brooks

Observation: We have a reliable GPS for navigating this world: offer love to everyone.

Your Response: It is so hard to . . . . .

MOVING ON Date_____

Song: "All of Me" Selah

Observation: Death brings us an uneasy knowledge we cannot get rid of.

Your Response: I'm sorry . . . . .

DENIAL   Date_____

Song: "Everywhere I Go" Tim Timmons

Observation: We must face the guilt we feel when others die and we do not.

Your Response: I want . . . . .

ANGER   Date_____

Song: "The Only Sound That Matters" Robert Plant

Observation: You have not failed, so do not despair in or distrust your life.

Your Response: I will never . . . . .

BROKEN HEART   Date_____

Song: "Turn It On, Turn It Up, Turn Me Loose" Dwight Yoakam

Observation: Continue to give to others, even if what you offer goes unnoticed and is not received.

Your Response: I did not know . . . . .

REMEMBERING   Date_____

Song: "Do I Ever Cross Your Mind" Joan Osborne

Observation: It is hard not to ruin today through memories of yesterday with you.

Your Response: The whole world can . . . . .

ACCEPTANCE   Date_____

Song: "He Walked on Water" Randy Travis

Observation: The heart has reasons we do not understand. Trust your heart and learn.

Your Response: I'm sorry . . . . .

MOVING ON   Date_____

Song: "Help Is on Its Way" The Little River Band

Observation: If God were not in control, we would be truly lost.

Your Response: My heart . . . . .

DENIAL   Date_____

Song: "I Don't Care" Robert Cray & Hi Rhythm

Observation: Denial will not save your life, but for a time it can help keep you sane.

Your Response: I don't care if . . . . .

ANGER   Date_____

Song: "Vaseline Machine Gun" Leo Kottke

Observation: Fearful people will buy everything the world is selling—sex, drugs, alcohol, busyness, violence, etc. The list is endless.

Your Response: I do not believe . . . . .

BROKEN HEART   Date_____

Song: "God Only Knows" The Beach Boys

Observation: Months after his aunt Mary died, six-year-old Daniel would say, "I don't know where I belong anymore."

Your Response: I was wrong . . . . .

REMEMBERING   Date_____

Song: "Mercy" Dave Matthews Band

Just what you wanted to hear: He's/she's in a better place.

Your Response: Time is . . . . .

ACCEPTANCE   Date_____

Song: "Everywhere I Go" Willie Nelson

Observation: Sunshine on a cold day makes everything feel better.

Your Response: How could you . . . . .

MOVING ON   Date_____

Song: "The Grass Is Blue" Norah Jones & Puss N Boots

Observation: To move on, you must trust the invisible reality to create your new life.

Your Response: My life is . . . . .

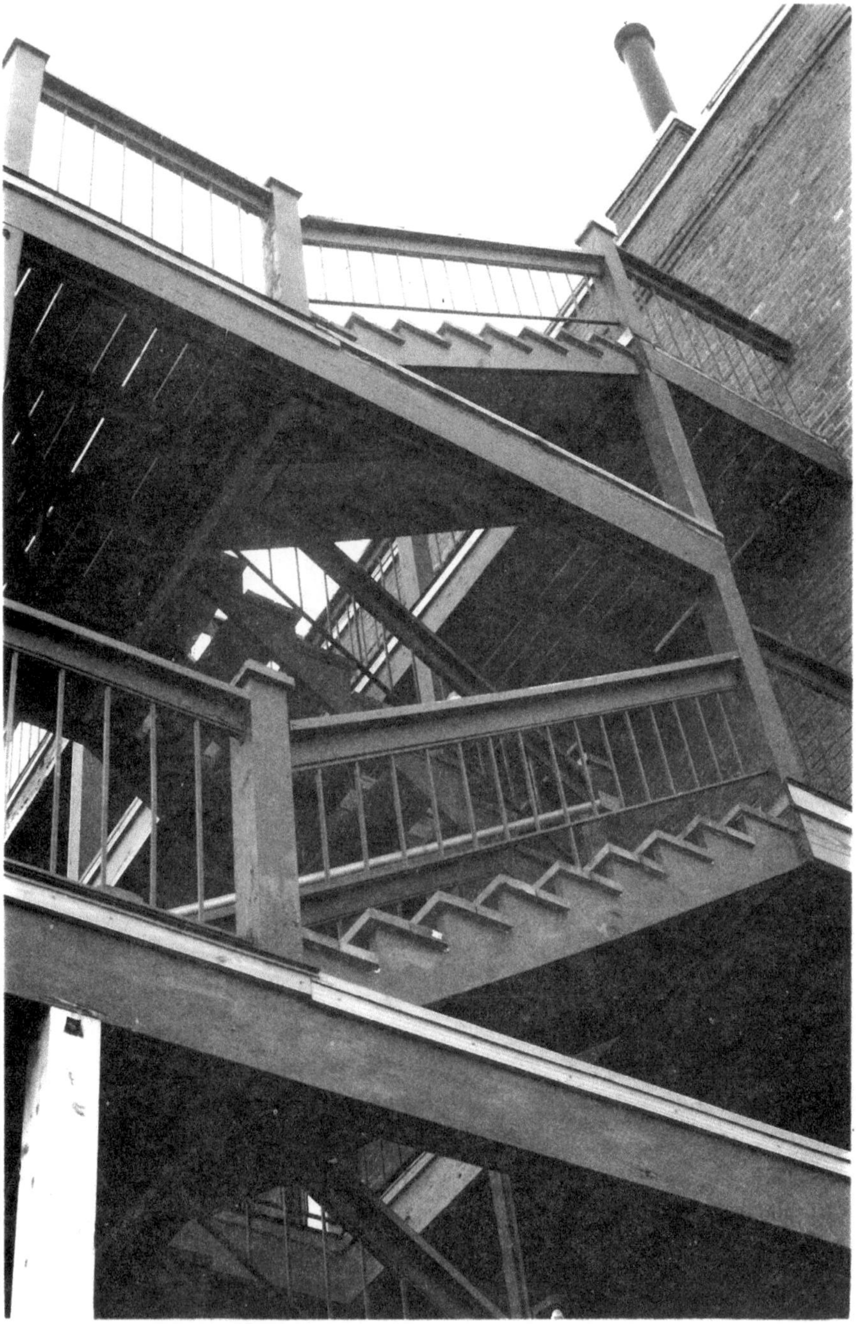

Altar the Pain

All that I know to be true
Does not Altar the pain.

I live as a toddler
Who cannot let go
Of wanting what
She cannot have
And so go play nicely with
The other children.

My heart refuses to
Let go.
My heart refuses to
Be reasonable.
My heart refuses to
Accept
That life goes on without
The one I love who brightened
Each day with his smile.

All that I know to be true
Does not Altar the pain.

And how can God heal
What I will not
Put on his Altar?

DENIAL   Date_____

Song: "I'm Hurtin'" Roy Orbison

Observation: People are like sharks; if we don't keep moving, we die.

Your Response: I don't care if . . . . .

ANGER   Date_____

Song: "Not Dark Yet" Bob Dylan

Observation: Bob says, if you are not having fun, you are doing it wrong.

Your Response: My days are so . . . . .

BROKEN HEART   Date_____

Song: "Alone Again (Naturally)" Diana Krall & Michael Buble

Observation: Does it help if you worry about your life?

Your Response: The world is . . . . .

REMEMBERING   Date_____

Song: "Driving Towards the Daylight" Joe Bonamassa

Observation: Do not let your life be defined by endless small troubles, or by big tragedies either.

Your Response: It makes me so angry that . . . . .

## ACCEPTANCE			Date_____

Song: "Thankful Heart" The Muppet Christmas Carol

Observation: Fun is the foundation of healing.

Your Response: It is so hard to . . . . .

## MOVING ON			Date_____

Song: "The Son Never Shines (On Closed Doors)" Flogging Molly

Observation: If we knew the future, would we live and enjoy today?

Your Response: I hate . . . . .

DENIAL   Date_____

Song: "I Take My Chances" Mary Chapin Carpenter

Observation: Is pain the greatest distraction from our feelings of fear, guilt, and unworthiness?

Your Response: My heart . . . . .

ANGER   Date_____

Song: "There In Your Heart" Beth Hart

Just what you wanted to hear: Everything happens for a reason.

Your Response: I love . . . . .

BROKEN HEART   Date_____

Song: "What I Had with You" John Conlee

Observation: Give me a new word to live up to. *Patience* is not working for me.

Your Response: I don't care if . . . . .

REMEMBERING   Date_____

Song: "Wasted on the Way" Crosby, Stills & Nash

Observation: The Ojibwa embrace the gifts of the seven grandfathers. Can you embrace Aakodewewin (bravery)?

Your Response: Please make it . . . . .

ACCEPTANCE   Date_____

Song: "Out of the Cold" Amos Lee

Observation: Nothing fills the human heart but love. Yet we try to live without it.

Your Response: The whole world can . . . . .

MOVING ON   Date_____

Song: "Oklahoma Wind" Tonic Sol-Fa

Observation: What noise of today am I using to hide the quiet joy of life's music?

Your Response: Just tell me . . . . .

DENIAL　　　　　　　　Date＿＿＿＿＿＿＿＿＿＿

Song: "The Last Thing I Needed First Thing This Morning" Willie Nelson

Observation: Hell is when you have nothing new in your life to love.

Your Response: Time is . . . . .

ANGER　　　　　　　　Date＿＿＿＿＿＿＿＿＿＿

Song: "Fire in the Sky" Nitty Gritty Dirt Band

Observation: Let God imagine you out of the box you are stuck in.

Your Response: It is so hard to . . . . .

BROKEN HEART   Date_____

Song: "I Wish It Would Rain" The Temptations

Observation: I want the magic spell that makes my lost love reappear.

Your Response: Don't tell me . . . . .

REMEMBERING   Date_____

Song: "Let Her Go" Passenger

Observation: It seems easier to die than to be left behind, so lost to love.

Your Response: I do not believe . . . . .

ACCEPTANCE   Date_____

Song: "Windows Are Rolled Down" Amos Lee

Observation: Your happiness is given to you, not to anyone else. Is this a curse or a blessing?

Your Response: I was wrong . . . . .

MOVING ON   Date_____

Song: "Forget Me Not" The Civil Wars

Observation: My story died with you. The new one makes no sense.

Your Response: The truth is . . . . .

DENIAL   Date_____

Song: "Silent Sea" KT Tunstall

Observation: In nothingness there is peace.

Your Response: Help me . . . . .

ANGER   Date_____

Song: "'A' is For Alligator" Ben Sidron

Observation: Does anyone understand how much I hate the new normal?

Your Response: The world is . . . . .

BROKEN HEART   Date_____

Song: "Shattered" Linda Ronstadt featuring Aaron Neville

Observation: The goal is finding everyone lovable, not just finding that special loved one.

Your Response: Life owes me . . . . .

REMEMBERING   Date_____

Song: "There Is a Reason" Alison Krauss & Union Station

Observation: Faith is not meant to be easy. It is a hard decision to trust God with every day you are given.

Your Observation: How could you . . . . .

ACCEPTANCE Date_____

Song: "Leading with Your Heart" Barbra Streisand

Observation: Grace is the will to want God more than you want happiness.

Your Response: I will never . . . . .

MOVING ON Date_____

Song: "Starting All Over Again" Israel Kamakawiwo'ole

Observation: God weaves people in and out of my life. How I touch them is my choice, with love or fear?

Your Response: Don't tell me . . . . .

DENIAL   Date_____

Song: "We All Need Saving" Tonic Sol-Fa

Observation: Denial makes it hard to trust God for the simple possibilities of your life.

Your Response: I'm sorry . . . . .

ANGER   Date_____

Song: "Graduation Day" Chris Isaak

Observation: Just because we cannot see God does not mean God does not see us.

Your Response: I should have told you . . . . .

BROKEN HEART   Date_____

Song: "Myself at Last" Graham Nash

Observation: I can offer you either my love or my fear.

Your Response: God is . . . . .

REMEMBERING   Date_____

Song: "Wilderness Road" Gino Vannelli

Observation: Before you can be found, you must know you are lost.

Your Response: I want . . . . .

ACCEPTANCE   Date_____

Song: "Fly" Celine Dion

Observation: Is death so scary that we can never talk about our dead loved ones?

Your Response: Why should I . . . . .

MOVING ON   Date_____

Song: "We'll Meet Again" Johnny Cash

Observation: We only control the ingredients to life, not the outcomes.

Your Response: God is . . . . .

"Welcome to Heaven's Gate. Press 1 for English, 2 for Spanish, 3 for French, 4 for Russian, 5 for Arabic, 6 for Chinese..."

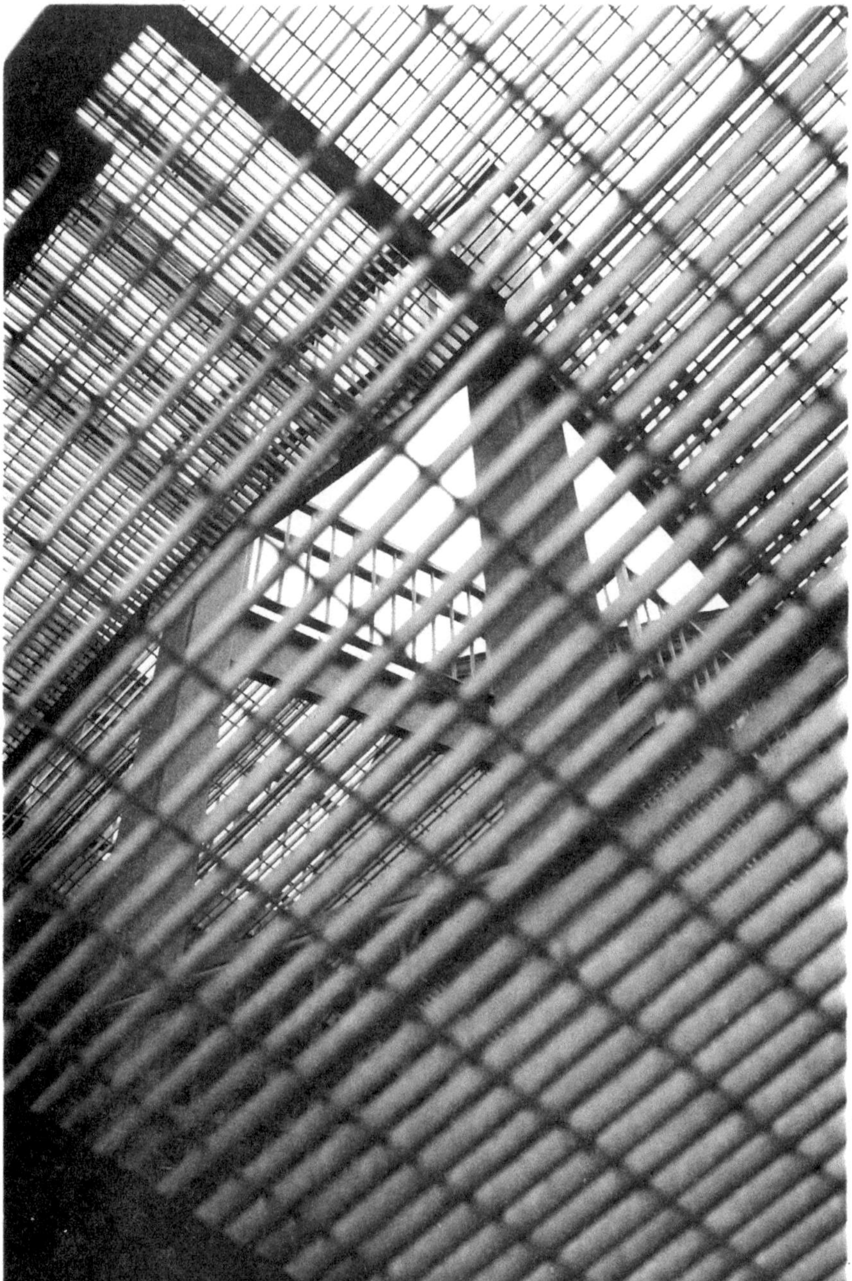

Hell

What is hell
But being a prisoner of
Your own mind?

So deeply frozen
In isolation
Not yet seeing the
Love offered
By the one
Sitting next
To you on the
Cold hard ground.

Love not running
Away,
Love looking for
The crack in your
Thoughts
That would let
Out the light
Walled in by fear.
Light that reflects
The soul of your
Would-be lover.

Can I sit on the edges
Of your hell
Lapped by the darkness
Of your mind?
With no way to
See myself?

Can I patiently wait
For you to come out
And play?

DENIAL Date_____

Song: "10 Rocks" Shelby Lynne

Observation: What would it mean if the world stopped when you died? Would you still be dead?

Your Response: Don't tell me . . . . .

ANGER Date_____

Song: "The Sound of Silence" Disturbed

Observation: Being alive is easier than *feeling* alive.

Your Response: I will never . . . . .

BROKEN HEART   Date_____

Song: "Your Love Stays With Me" Shelby Lynne

Just what you wanted to hear: Walk it off. Seriously, go out the front door and walk.

Your Response: God owes me . . . . .

REMEMBERING   Date_____

Song: "Unforgettable" Nat King Cole

Observation: I am forever connected to all that is, including you.

Your Response: If only . . . . .

ACCEPTANCE   Date_____

Song: "Love God - And Everyone Else" Al Green

Observation: Look around you. Would you really trade this present for the past?

Your Response: I hate . . . . .

MOVING ON   Date_____

Song: "As Long As I Have a Song" Beth Hart

Observation: The real question seems to be, why am I not enough for myself?

Your Response: It is so hard . . . . .

DENIAL Date _____

Song: "All My Love Is Gone" Lyle Lovett

Observation: Deny it again and again until the illusion you hold is seen as worthless.

Your Response: I don't care if . . . . .

ANGER Date _____

Song: "Way Down We Go" KALEO

Observation: The dead are like cats who will not come when you call them, even when they know their names and love you.

Your Response: Why should I . . . . .

BROKEN HEART   Date_____

Song: "All Who Are Thirsty" Brenton Brown

Observation: Hell is living with random hope.

Your Response: How could you . . . . .

REMEMBERING   Date_____

Song: "Old Blue Chair" Kenny Chesney

Observation: Love has ferociously perfect moments. They can heal the past.

Your Response: My life is . . . . .

ACCEPTANCE   Date_____

Song: "Smile" Nat King Cole

Observation: We are an honest witness to our feelings when we don't try to change them.

Your Response: God is . . . . .

MOVING ON   Date_____

Song: "Why Walk When You Can Fly" Mary Chapin Carpenter

Observation: What has slipped through your fingers leaves only the shadow of your empty hand. Can you still love it?

Your Response: I will never . . . . .

DENIAL   Date_____

Song: "I Guess That's Why They Call It the Blues" Elton John

Observation: Best cat poster ever: The World Depends on What You Believe.

Your Response: Time is . . . . .

ANGER   Date_____

Song: "Crash This Train" Joshua James

Observation: If death is the price we pay for enjoying the banquet of life, did you leave a big tip?

Your Response: Help me . . . . .

BROKEN HEART   Date_____

Song: "Down to the River to Pray" Alison Krauss & Union Station

Observation: If you live only in hope for tomorrow, you may miss meeting God today.

Your Response: The whole world can . . . . .

REMEMBERING   Date_____

Song: "Holdin' on to Yesterday" Ambrosia

Observation: You can spend a lifetime saying goodbye.

Your Response: I'm sorry . . . . .

## ACCEPTANCE				Date_____

Song: "To Comfort You" Bette Midler

Observation: To know love, you must create joy out of sorrow.

Your Response: Don't tell me . . . . .

## MOVING ON				Date_____

Song: "The River" Garth Brooks

Observation: You only really love those you are willing to set free.

Your Response: I love . . . . .

DENIAL   Date_____

Song: "Go out Swingin" Alison Scott

Observation: Even the useless gesture can make a difference.

Your Response: My days are so . . . . .

ANGER   Date_____

Song: "Nothin' Works" Leo Kottke

Observation: Death is a heart transplant with no anesthesia.

Your Response: I did not know . . . . .

BROKEN HEART   Date_____

Song: "Sad, Sad Music" Dwight Yoakam

Observation: The sources of life and love are still in your hands.

Your Response: Show me . . . . .

REMEMBERING   Date_____

Song: "Marching Soldiers" Tonic Sol-Fa

Observation: To honor our loved ones we must braid the good and bad memories together.

Your Response: Please make it . . . . .

ACCEPTANCE Date_____

Song: "On the Sunny Side of the Street" Louis Armstrong

Observation: Only when we look forward do we trace the hand of God weaving our lives.

Your Response: The world is . . . . .

MOVING ON Date_____

Song: "Talking to My Angel" Melissa Etheridge

Observation: I feel like a withered winter apple still hanging on a tree. Will spring bring me life?

Your Response: Help me . . . . .

DENIAL   Date_____

Song: "Since You Been Gone" The Rad Trads

Observation: The Ojibwa embrace the gifts of the seven grandfathers. Can you embrace Debwewin (truth)?

Your Response: I want . . . . .

ANGER   Date_____

Song: "Born with a Broken Heart" Kenny Wayne Shepherd

Observation: To live is to impose order on your death-leveled life.

Your Response: I was wrong . . . . .

BROKEN HEART   Date_____

Song: "Endless Sleep" Leo Kottke

Observation: Love is for those brave enough to be left behind.

Your Response: The truth . . . . .

REMEMBERING   Date_____

Song: "I Will Remember You" Sarah McLachlan

Observation: The only thing that can trap me is my own mind.

Your Response: My heart . . . . .

ACCEPTANCE   Date_____

Song: "Last Train" Arlo Guthrie

Observation: My mind is the tool that changes the world.

Your Response: I believe . . . . .

MOVING ON   Date_____

Song: "Instead" Madeleine Peyroux

Just what you wanted to hear: If only you had made better choices.

Your Response: Give me back . . . . .

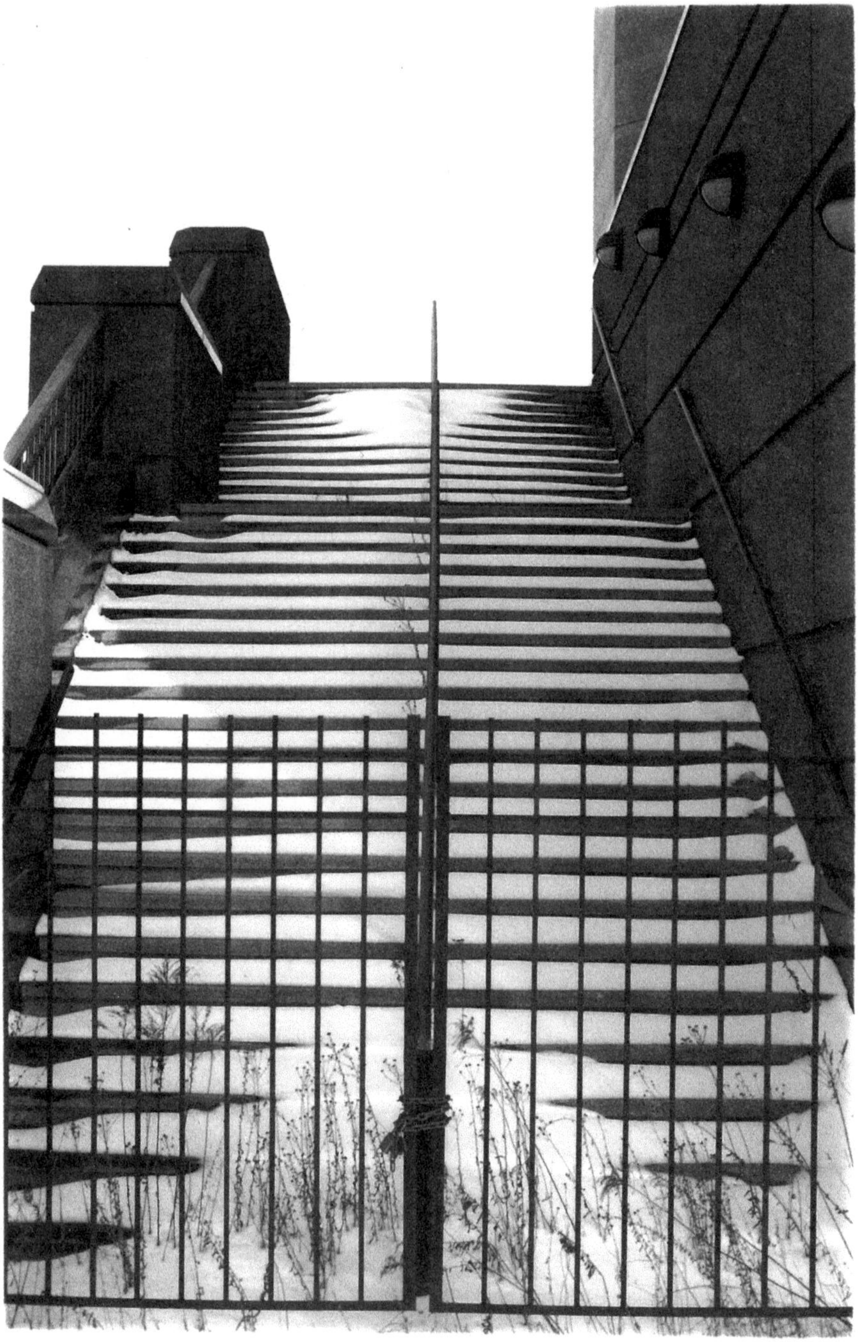

Sanctuary

The sanctuary in my heart,
Where love once danced,
Is empty.

It echoes and
Wants no comfort,
No happy distractions,
No substitutes,
No warmth of other loves.

It wants just the dead.
The dead more real than the living.

I am felled by
Emptiness wanting
What it cannot have.

DENIAL   Date_____

Song: "New Way to Fly" Garth Brooks

Observation: Our bad behavior tries to defy God's love for us.

Your Response: God is . . . . .

ANGER   Date_____

Song: "Some Town Somewhere" Kenny Chesney

Observation: God cannot bring His life to you if you are always holding on to your version.

Your Response: I will never . . . . .

BROKEN HEART   Date_____

Song: "Don't Know How (Not to Love You)" Uncle Kracker

Observation: Feeling lost is like cat fur—you find it everywhere.

Your Response: Just tell me . . . . .

REMEMBERING   Date_____

Song: "For a Dancer" Emmylou Harris & Linda Ronstadt

Observation: Dancing with you is all I ever wanted to do.

Your Response: Time is . . . . .

ACCEPTANCE   Date_____

Song: "Hungry Heart" Bruce Springsteen

Observation: Does acceptance become tolerable if bitterness is the only other option?

Your Response: I did not know . . . . .

MOVING ON   Date_____

Song: "Piece of My Heart" Keri Noble

Observation: Bring your two loaves and five fish, and let God feed your world.

Your Response: I'm sorry . . . . .

DENIAL   Date_____

Song: "Body & Soul" Stan Getz

Observation: How much work are you doing just to hide from God's love?

Your Response: I should have told you . . . . .

ANGER   Date_____

Song: "Sympathy for the Devil" The Rolling Stones

Observation: There are fates worse than loneliness; even God is lonely.

Your Response: Why should I . . . . .

BROKEN HEART   Date_____

Song: "Sea of Heartbreak" Jimmy Buffett & George Strait

Observation: Is life fair if everyone gets a portion of death?

Your Response: I hate . . . . .

REMEMBERING   Date_____

Song: "Crazy" Diane Schuur

Observation: The feelings of our hearts are the center of our lives.

Your Response: If only . . . . .

ACCEPTANCE   Date_____

Song: "They Dance Alone (Gueca Solo)" Sting

Observation: If we are lucky, the truth will capture us and not let us go.

Your Response: My heart . . . . .

MOVING ON   Date_____

Song: "Dust to Dust" The Civil Wars

Just what you wanted to hear: You are free now.

Your Response: God owes me . . . . .

DENIAL   Date_____

Song: "Groaning the Blues" Eric Clapton

Observation: Give yourself permission to find joy and not just pain in life.

Your Response: It is hard to . . . . .

ANGER   Date_____

Song: "Thistle & Weeds" Mumford & Sons

Observation: There are many things one can do while raging at life.

Your Response: Give me back . . . . .

BROKEN HEART   Date_____

Song: "Tin Man" Miranda Lambert

Observation: Love your wounds and brokenness, and God's light will shine through.

Your Response: Please make it . . . . .

REMEMBERING   Date_____

Song: "Where Is Love Now" Nickel Creek

Observation: We need a national "Speak of the Dead" day so we share our memories.

Your Response: Help me . . . . .

ACCEPTANCE   Date_____

Song: "Cat's in the Cradle" Harry Chapin

Observation: How you live your life is between you and God.

Your Response: How could you . . . . .

MOVING ON   Date_____

Song: "Lighter Shade of Blue" Shelby Lynne

Observation: I have forgotten how to be the only thing to be: a child of God.

Your Response: Don't tell me . . . . .

DENIAL Date_____

Song: "Storm Warning" Rodney Crowell

Observation: A heart full of the things of this world seldom has room for joy.

Your Response: I did not know that . . . . .

ANGER Date_____

Song: "All My Tears" Selah

Observation: Whatever your brain is screaming at you about—let it go. You are good enough.

Your Response: I was wrong . . . . .

BROKEN HEART   Date_____

Song: "The Only Thing Wrong" Jamie O'Neal

Observation: Use fear to wake up your life, not to shut it down.

Your Response: Will anyone ever . . . . .

REMEMBERING   Date_____

Song: "Goodbye My Friend" Linda Ronstadt featuring Aaron Neville

Observation: Honor your dead by getting your life together. This is how you will know you were worthy of their love.

Your Response: The whole world can . . . . .

ACCEPTANCE　　　　　Date_____

Song: "With a Little Help from My Friends" The Beatles

Observation: Do you love yourself enough to live alone?

Your Response: I want . . . . .

MOVING ON　　　　　Date_____

Song: "Shine It All Around" Robert Plant

Observation: May God's love dance with me.

Your Observation: My life is so . . . . .

DENIAL   Date_____

Song: "It Feels Like Rain" Aaron Neville

Observation: If peace comes from being certain, what are you certain of?

Your Response: I love . . . . .

ANGER   Date_____

Song: "I Won't Back Down" Dawn Landes

Observation: Maybe someday "How can this have happened?" becomes "OK, this is what happened."

Your Response: Show me . . . . .

BROKEN HEART Date_____

Song: "Thinking out Loud" Ed Sheeran

Observation: I miss being able to make my life around you.

Your Response: My days are so . . . . .

REMEMBERING Date_____

Song: "Hold On" Shawn Colvin

Observation: Compassion is feeling deeply and giving generously with no expectations of reward.

Your Response: The truth is . . . . .

ACCEPTANCE   Date_____

Song: "I Bid You Goodnight" Aaron Neville

Observation: God has remembered you; do you remember God?

Your Response: It makes me so angry that . . . . .

MOVING ON   Date_____

Song: "Love's Gonna Live Here" Martina McBride

Observation: You will live through the mysteries of your life, so own them.

Your Response: Will anyone ever . . . . .

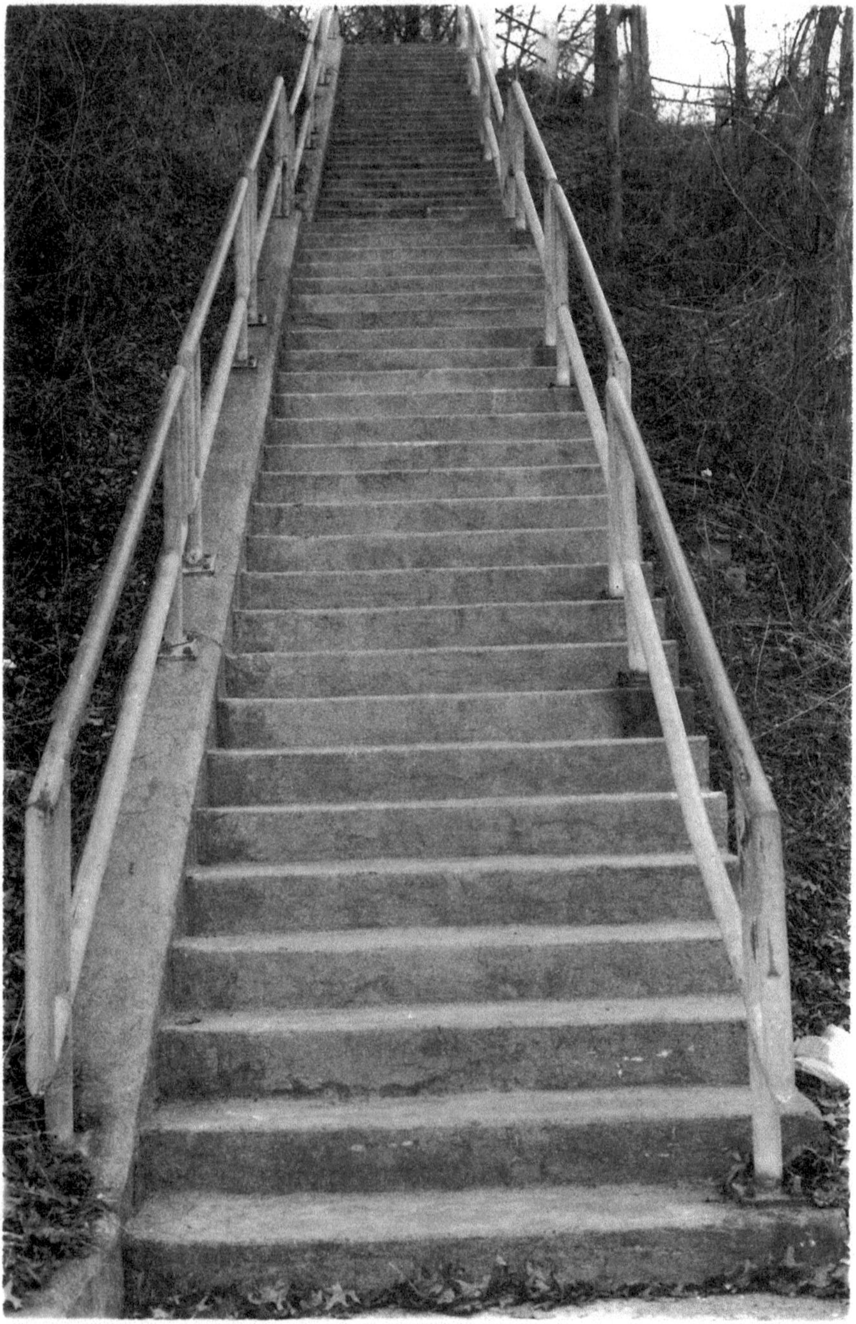

Enough

More of what
You don't want
Is never enough
To be happy with yourself.

And I don't want to
Be without you,
So more without you
Is not enough.

I am not enough
Without you.
Was I ever enough
Before you?

How am I not enough
For myself?
Worthy of breathing
Another day.

Why God did You bring
This new man
Into my Life?

Was it just to show
Me that I am not
Enough for another
Man to love,
If I cannot be
Enough for myself?

It runs deep,
This curse of
Cain and Abel,
This need to be special.

And I cry
enough. Already.

DENIAL   Date_____

Song: "I Will" Alison Krauss featuring Tony Furtado

Observation: I am alive only in this exact moment. I can only live now.

Your Response: The truth . . . . .

ANGER   Date_____

Song: "Cup of Sorrow" Amos Lee

Observation: We all look away from death.

Your Response: If only . . . . .

BROKEN HEART   Date_____

Song: "Ain't No Sunshine" Bill Withers

Observation: The truth brings you a braid of darkness and light, sorrow and joy.

Your Response: I should have told you . . . . .

REMEMBERING   Date_____

Song: "He Never Failed Me Yet" Robert Robinson

Observation: Are you ready to live free from illusions?

Your Response: I want . . . . .

ACCEPTANCE   Date_____

Song: "I Can Let Go Now" Tommy Emmanuel & John Knowles

Observation: Your heart always has room to give more love.

Your Response: Why should I . . . . .

MOVING ON   Date_____

Song: "Go Light Your World" Shaun Johnson Big Band Experience

Observation: Life loves those who embrace and struggle with uncertainty.

Your Response: My heart . . . . .

DENIAL   Date_____

Song: "Gone, Gone, Gone (Done Moved On)" Robert Plant & Alison Krauss

Observation: Here I am again, over my head, in a mess, and scared.

Your Response: The whole world can . . . . .

ANGER   Date_____

Song: "Joy" Beth Hart & Joe Bonamassa

Observation: If you can't shed your skin, you cannot live and grow.

Your Response: Give me back my . . . . .

BROKEN HEART   Date_____

Song: "Make You Feel My Love" Bob Dylan

Observation: New skin hurts.

Your Response: Just tell me . . . . .

REMEMBERING   Date_____

Song: "Survivor" Robert Cray

Observation: Reality comes when all illusions are gone and you are no longer innocent.

Your Response: How could you . . . . .

ACCEPTANCE   Date_____

Song: "Somewhere Along the Way" Nat King Cole

Observation: God teaches us how to neutralize pain, not multiply it.

Your Response: Please make it . . . . .

MOVING ON   Date_____

Song: "I Stand" Idina Menzel

Observation: The Ojibwa embrace the gifts of the seven grandfathers. Can you embrace Bimaadiziwin (a good life)?

Your Response: Don't tell me . . . . .

DENIAL   Date_____

Song: "Change the World" Eric Clapton

Observation: We are always free to ignore the joy that comes to our lives.

Your Response: I love . . . . .

ANGER   Date_____

Song: "Dying Anyway" Ben Sidran

Observation: How can anything in my life redeem the loss of my loved one?

Your Response: I don't care if . . . . .

BROKEN HEART   Date_____

Song: "In My Life" Johnny Cash

Just what you wanted to hear: You will get used to the new normal.

Your Response: I hate . . . . .

REMEMBERING   Date_____

Song: "I Am" Crowder

Observation: Name the pain that you want to hold on to, so then you can let it go.

Your Response: I will never . . . . .

ACCEPTANCE   Date_____

Song: "When the Curtain Comes Down" Diana Krall

Observation: The leap of faith is jumping when you cannot see the landing.

Your Response: I'm sorry . . . . .

MOVING ON   Date_____

Song: "Move (Keep Walkin')" TobyMac

Observation: Become the person you needed most when you were younger.

Your Response: God is . . . . .

DENIAL   Date_____

Song: "Nothing You Can't Lose" The Steel Wheels

Just what you wanted to hear: God is punishing you for something you did.

Your Response: Help me . . . . .

ANGER   Date_____

Song: "St. James Infirmary" Arlo Guthrie

Observation: Only evil runs straight over others to achieve its ends.

Your Response: I do not believe . . . . .

BROKEN HEART   Date_____

Song: "What Are You Gonna Do About Me" Buddy Guy featuring Beth Hart

Observation: "How much will you work to find what you want?" is the basic question of life.

Your Response: Give me back . . . . .

REMEMBERING   Date_____

Song: "The Greatest Man I Never Knew" Reba McEntire

Observation: Belief is the foundation of everything in life, good or bad.

Your Response: How could you . . . . .

ACCEPTANCE   Date_____

Song: "Nobody Wins" Kris Kristofferson

Observation: You will not understand why life happens as it does. To believe otherwise will keep you feeling crazy.

Your Response: I was wrong . . . . .

MOVING ON   Date_____

Song: "Love Is the Law" The New Standards

Observation: Do not despise the small beginnings. Even David was a lowly shepherd before he became the mighty king.

Your Response: I'm sorry . . . . .

DENIAL   Date_____

Song: "Where Are You Christmas?" Faith Hill

Observation: Anyone can die. Living is what takes effort.

Your Response: I hate . . . . .

ANGER   Date_____

Song: "Four Walls" Jim Reeves

Observation: If you only allow one person's smile to love you, you miss the smiles of everyone else.

Your Response: Time is . . . . .

BROKEN HEART   Date_____

Song: "Heart of Stone" Dwight Yoakam

Observation: Don't trade what is real for what isn't.

Your Response: Will anyone ever . . . . .

REMEMBERING   Date_____

Song: "You Still Touch Me" Sting

Observation: Most of our best memories are unintentional.

Your Response: I did not know . . . . .

ACCEPTANCE   Date_____

Song: "Find My Way Back to My Heart" Alison Krauss & Union Station

Observation: If you are lucky, being alive means you are always outgrowing yourself.

Your Response: My days are so . . . .

MOVING ON   Date_____

Song: "Let It Grow" Eric Clapton

Observation: Make a list of small things you must do each day, like smile and laugh. Then do them every day.

Your Response: Just tell me . . . . .

"Welcome to Heaven's Gate. To access your personal account, please enter your user name and password at the prompts."

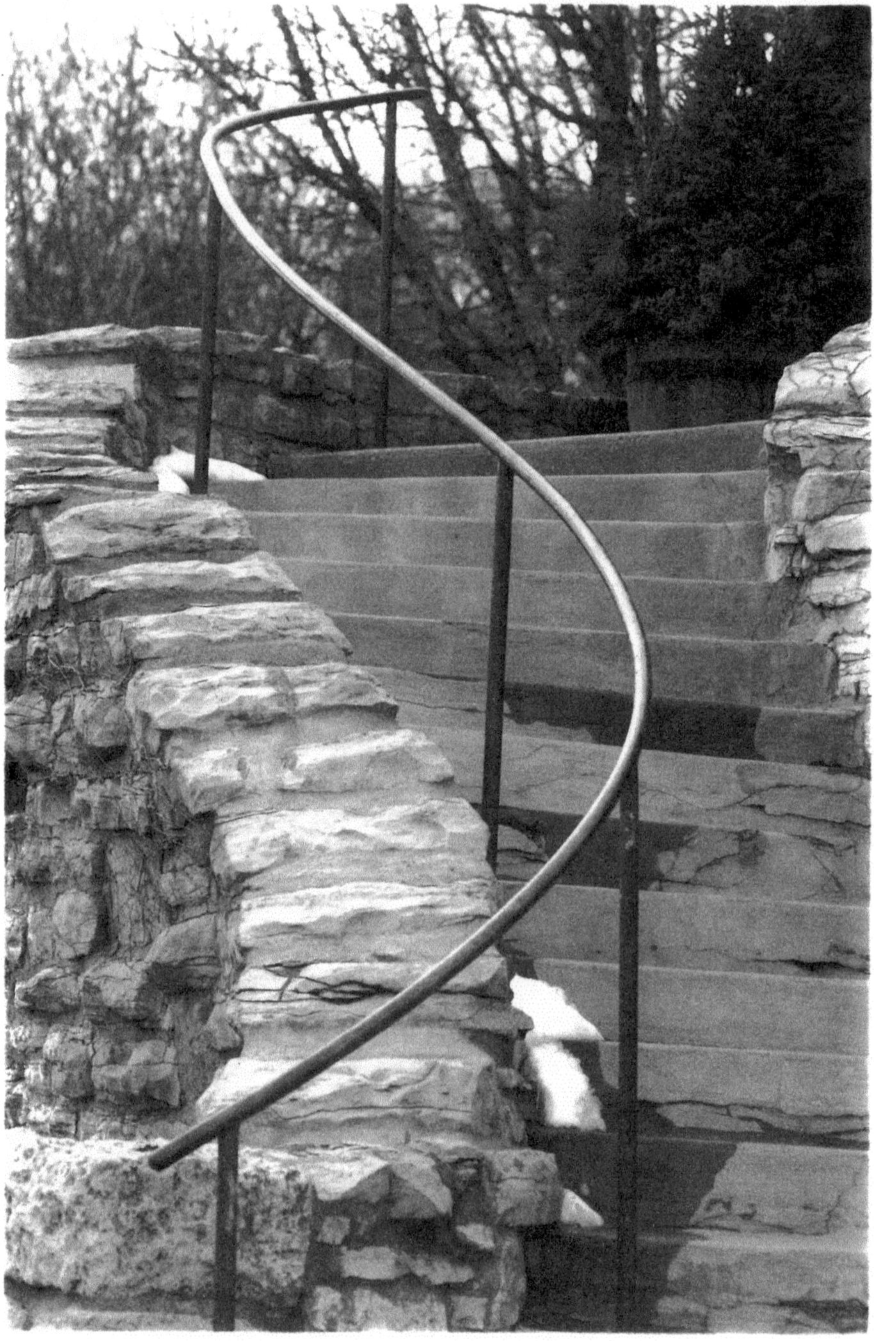

Sorry

I can say
I am sorry,
I did not understand,
I was wrong.

But I cannot say
Help me.

Those words
Stick in my throat
And feel
Like spears in my heart.

I defy you to
Make me need you like
I needed him to breathe.

I have carved a place for you
In my life, safely tucked in
A corner of my outer walls,
Where you will not
hurt me when you leave.

And you will leave.

For I am the refuge where
Souls come to heal,
Where love comes for a time
And then moves on.

Foolish me, I mourn
Never stepping into the
Same river twice.

DENIAL   Date_____

Song: "Coming Around Again" Carly Simon

Observation: Death brings you the darkness, now you must find the light.

Your Response: I hate . . . . .

ANGER   Date_____

Song: "Why Worry" Dire Straits

Observation: When you learn that today is enough, peace of mind will follow.

Your Response: The world is . . . . .

BROKEN HEART   Date_____

Song: "A Broken Wing" Crystal Bowersox

Observation: Wanting the world to stop is mostly wanting your mind to shut up.

Your Response: My days are so . . . . .

REMEMBERING   Date_____

Song: "Don't Let It Bring You Down" Bela Fleck & Abigail Washburn

Observation: Death is one sure thing that stops time, for everyone.

Your Response: Will anyone ever . . . . .

ACCEPTANCE Date_____

Song: "The Light in Your Eyes" LeAnn Rimes

Observation: Healing comes from loving all of life, and life requires death.

Your Response: It is so hard to . . . . .

MOVING ON Date_____

Song: "A Million Years Ago" Adele

Observation: God's love for you does not live in the past. Look for it today.

Your Response: I should have told you . . . . .

DENIAL   Date_____

Song: "Broken Bones" KALEO

Observation: Chaos may be the voice of God, but I still long for quiet.

Your Response: Life owes me . . . . .

ANGER   Date_____

Song: "Angola Bound" Aaron Neville

Observation: Do you trust the light of life enough to die?

Your Response: If only . . . . .

BROKEN HEART   Date_____

Song: "When You Come Back to Me Again" Garth Brooks

Observation: Can I have just one more day with you?

Your Response: I love . . . . .

REMEMBERING   Date_____

Song: "Everything Is Broken" Kenny Wayne Shepherd

Observation: Being loved by you made me feel alive and relevant.

Your Response: I did not know . . . . .

ACCEPTANCE   Date_____

Song: "Shelter or the Storm" Sarah Morris

Observation: How can I accept my new life when I feel useless, unwanted?

Your Response: My life is . . . . .

MOVING ON   Date_____

Song: "American Tune" Shawn Colvin

Observation: A world of small loves can feel safer than a world where anything is possible and love comes as it will.

Your Response: I should have told you . . . . .

## DENIAL	Date_____

Song: "Timeless" Selah

Just what you wanted to hear: You need to move on with your life.

Your Response: Will anyone ever . . . . .

## ANGER	Date_____

Song: "Lonely with a Broken Heart" Chris Isaak

Observation: How long before I am done with feeling tragic?

Your Response: The whole world can . . . . .

BROKEN HEART   Date_____

Song: "I Can't Stop Loving You" Martina McBride

Observation: The world, my whole life, simply feels wrong without you.

Your Response: Time is . . . . .

REMEMBERING   Date_____

Song: "Perfect Moment" Art Garfunkel featuring Buddy Mondlock

Observation: Remembering you is easy. Finding someone who wants to share those memories is hard.

Your Response: The truth is . . . . .

ACCEPTANCE Date_____

Song: "Wouldn't Be So Bad" Alison Krauss & Union Station

Observation: I now understand why some people quit living in the bleak face of death.

Your Response: My heart . . . . .

MOVING ON Date_____

Song: "Bang Bang Boom Boom" Beth Hart

Observation: There seems to be no moving on. There is only walking bigger circles around death.

Your Response: I want . . . . .

DENIAL Date_____

Song: "Drivin' Nails in My Coffin" Ernest Tubb

Observation: Depression lives between conceding and accepting.

Your Response: Give me back . . . . .

ANGER Date_____

Song: "Somebody That I Used to Know" Gotye & Kimbra

Observation: Acceptance does not need the weapon of hope.

Your Response: God is . . . . .

BROKEN HEART   Date_____

Song: "I Love" Tom T. Hall

Observation: Life is mostly like the drive-thru. You must order, but you don't always get it right.

Your Response: Help me . . . . .

REMEMBERING   Date_____

Song: "Come to Jesus" Mindy Smith

Observation: You slipped like sunshine through my fingers. I see only the shadow of my empty hand.

Your Response: Show me . . . . .

ACCEPTANCE   Date_____

Song: "Train Home" Chris Smither

Observation: When we stop and quit interfering with our own lives, God's answer can be found.

Your Response: I do not believe . . . . .

MOVING ON   Date_____

Song: "In Hell I'll Be in Good Company" The Dead South

Observation: If you have never known pain, can you honestly say you are happy?

Your Response: Don't tell me . . . . .

DENIAL   Date_____

Song: "No Hard Feelings" The Avett Brothers

Observation: Trusting God for your supply allows you to give generously.

Your Response: The world is . . . . .

ANGER   Date_____

Song: "It's Four in the Morning" Feron Young

Observation: My tummy hurts. Where is peace now that there is death?

Your Response: My days are so . . . . .

BROKEN HEART   Date_____

Song: "Shahdaroba" Roy Orbison

Observation: Trust is a hard and rocky road without faith to light the way.

Your Response: I was wrong . . . . .

REMEMBERING   Date_____

Song: "Let It Go" Bela Fleck & Abigail Washburn

Observation: Life is full of unconventional angels, like the gift of Dilly Bars to the dying appetite.

Your Response: I don't care if . . . . .

ACCEPTANCE   Date_____

Song: "Better Than Home" Beth Hart

Observation: Why don't you come when I call you?

Your Response: Just tell me . . . . .

MOVING ON   Date_____

Song: "The Land of Milk and Honey" Kelley Hunt

Observation: When life seems to give us less, we can grow it into more.

Your Response: It makes me so angry . . . . .

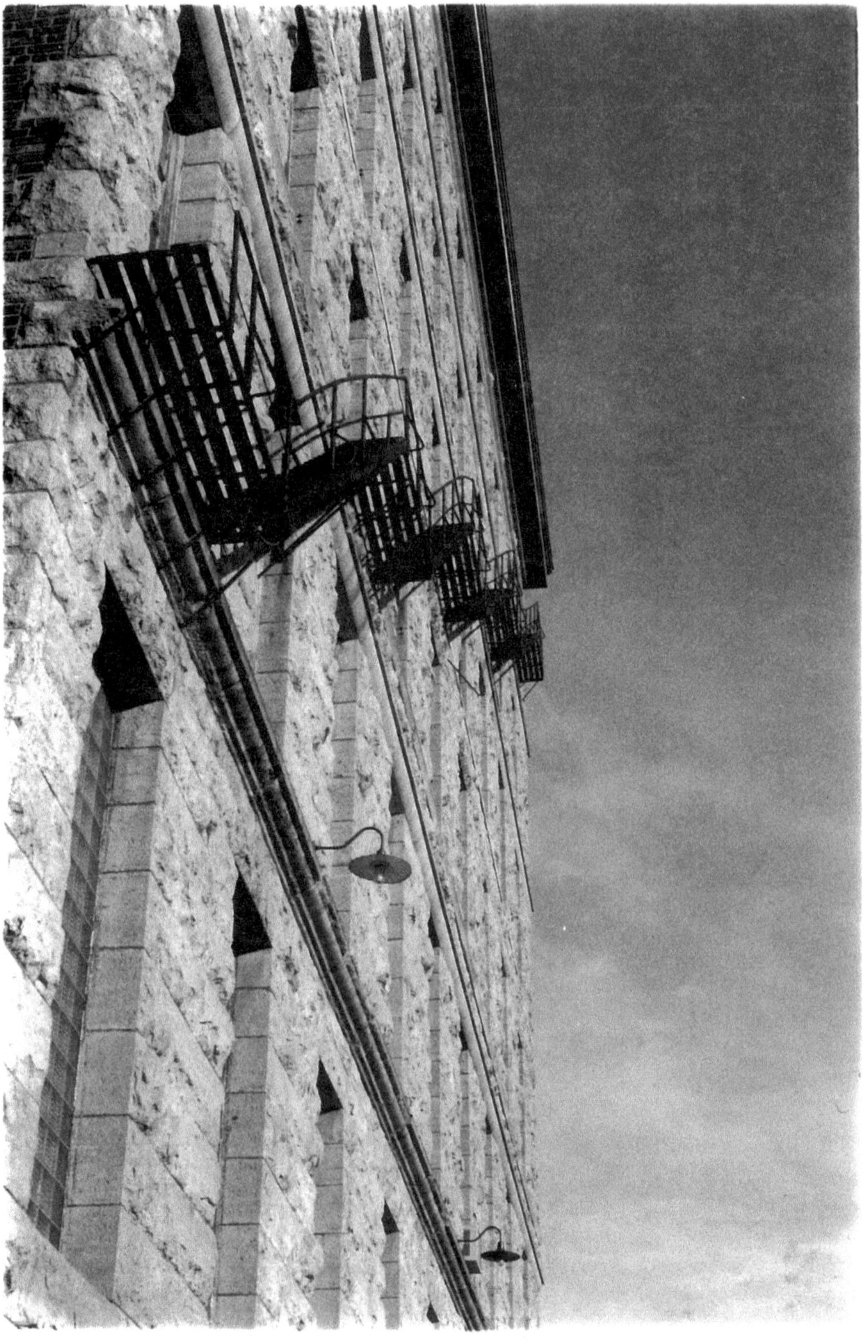

From Carly's Song

Carly sings there's more room
In your heart when it is broken.
So mine must be huge.

And yet I wonder if there is
Room for you
Here in my heart of grief.
And yet the universe brought you
To my door, and me to yours.

If my heart is broken again, it will
Be big enough to hold the vast cold
Vacuum of space.

And no sun's warmth
Will heal me then.

DENIAL   Date_____

Song: "Call the Man" Celine Dion

Just what you wanted to hear: It is what it is.

Your Response: I love . . . . .

ANGER   Date_____

Song: "Last Call to Heaven" The White Buffalo

Observation: Would it really be better if you could punish someone for your loss?

Your Response: Why should I . . . . .

BROKEN HEART Date_____

Song: "Losing My Faith" Jelly Roll

Observation: Don't be embarrassed to rely on God to make your impossible grief possible.

Your Response: Please make it . . . . .

REMEMBERING Date_____

Song: "This Life" John Paul White

Observation: Sometimes we live invisible like God: quiet, patient, and lonely.

Your Response: I will never . . . . .

ACCEPTANCE   Date_____

Song: "Life Is Beautiful" Keb' Mo'

Observation: To know love, you must also know loss.

Your Response: It is so hard to . . . . .

MOVING ON   Date_____

Song: "I'm in a Hurry (And Don't Know Why)" Alabama

Observation: The darkness can be gone when you turn on the light.

Your Response: It makes me so angry that . . . . .

DENIAL   Date_____

Song: "Scrape Me Off the Ceiling" The Steel Wheels

Observation: In life, there are times that are going to hurt no matter what you do. This is one of them.

Your Response: The truth is . . . . .

ANGER   Date_____

Song: "Coal War" Joshua James

Observation: The Ojibwa embrace the gifts of the seven grandfathers. Can you embrace Nibwaakawin (wisdom)?

Your Response: Don't tell me . . . . .

BROKEN HEART   Date_____

Song: "All You Got Is a Song" Amos Lee

Observation: Today is supposed to be enough. Why is it still not enough?

Your Response: I'm sorry . . . . .

REMEMBERING   Date_____

Song: "If Not For You" Bob Dylan

Observation: Grief is the stairway you climb to nowhere you want to go.

Your Response: Show me . . . . .

ACCEPTANCE   Date_____

Song: "Heal Over" KT Tunstall

Just what you wanted to hear: You are so brave and positive about life.

Your Response: I do not believe . . . . .

MOVING ON   Date_____

Song: "She Just Wants to Dance" Keb' Mo'

Observation: Death ended our story, and I do not know how to write mine.

Your Response: It is so hard to . . . . .

DENIAL   Date_____

Song: "Lie to Me" Jonny Lang

Observation: I wonder if the newly dead change the world by affecting the still living?

Your Response: How could you . . . . .

ANGER   Date_____

Song: "Wrestling With Angels" Gino Vannelli

Observation: Grief is the black foggy cloud in your head that hides all of your thoughts.

Your Response: I don't care if . . . . .

BROKEN HEART   Date_____

Song: "Not Easy" Alex Da Kid featuring X Ambassadors, Elle King, and Wiz Khalifa

Observation: The human heart rules.

Your Response: Please make it . . . . .

REMEMBERING   Date_____

Song: "Good Grief" Dessa

Observation: Most days, remembering your love is not enough.

Your Response: The world is . . . . .

ACCEPTANCE   Date_____

Song: "Let Your Loss Be Your Lesson" Robert Plant & Alison Krauss

Observation: Faith is agreeing with what God says is true of my life.

Your Response: I should have told you . . . . .

MOVING ON   Date_____

Song: "Come What May" JD Souther

Observation: Your story is all that remains of you. It was a wondrous story.

Your Response: The whole world can . . . . .

DENIAL   Date_____

Song: "Highwayman" The Highwaymen

Observation: When denial begins to fade, you will see your life more clearly.

Your Response: My life is so . . . . .

ANGER   Date_____

Song: "Wonder Why We Ever Go Home" Jimmy Buffett

Observation: Impermanence is the ultimate gift of life.

Your Response: My heart . . . . .

BROKEN HEART   Date_____

Song: "Dreaming with a Broken Heart" John Mayer

Observation: Evil hunts for the hungry heart.

Your Response: I want . . . . .

REMEMBERING   Date_____

Song: "You Got Me Singing" Leonard Cohen

Observation: Without love, the heart feels only the darkness.

Your Response: God owes me . . . . .

ACCEPTANCE   Date_____

Song: "How Was I to Know" Reba McEntire

Observation: I am not here to argue with God.

Your Response: My days are so . . . . .

_____

MOVING ON   Date_____

Song: "Don't Ever Be Blue" Davell Crawford featuring Steve Riley

Observation: The Scottish word *thrawn* means a person has a pride that won't let them quit. You need thrawn in your life.

Your Observation: I will never . . . . .

DENIAL   Date_____

Song: "No Place to Hide" Alison Krauss & Union Station

Observation: I am forever connected to all that is, including you.

Your Response: I hate . . . . .

ANGER   Date_____

Song: "Let You Down" Dave Matthews Band

Observation: Where is God's will in the endless chaos?

Your Response: Will anyone ever . . . . .

BROKEN HEART   Date⎯⎯⎯⎯⎯⎯⎯⎯⎯⎯⎯⎯⎯⎯

Song: "Simplify" Kelley Hunt

Observation: The only love missing from any situation is mine.

Your Response: If only . . . . .

REMEMBERING   Date⎯⎯⎯⎯⎯⎯⎯⎯⎯⎯⎯⎯⎯⎯

Song: "Timshel" Mumford & Sons

Observation: The dead know what you do, what you give, and what you love.

Your Response: I was wrong . . . . .

ACCEPTANCE   Date_____

Song: "Why Me" Kris Kristofferson

Observation: Let God's love for today outweigh your grief for the past.

Your Response: I did not know . . . . .

MOVING ON   Date_____

Song: "Hard Times" Front Porch String Band

Observation: Now that you're gone, where is the love that will grant me purpose?

Your Response: Why should I . . . . .

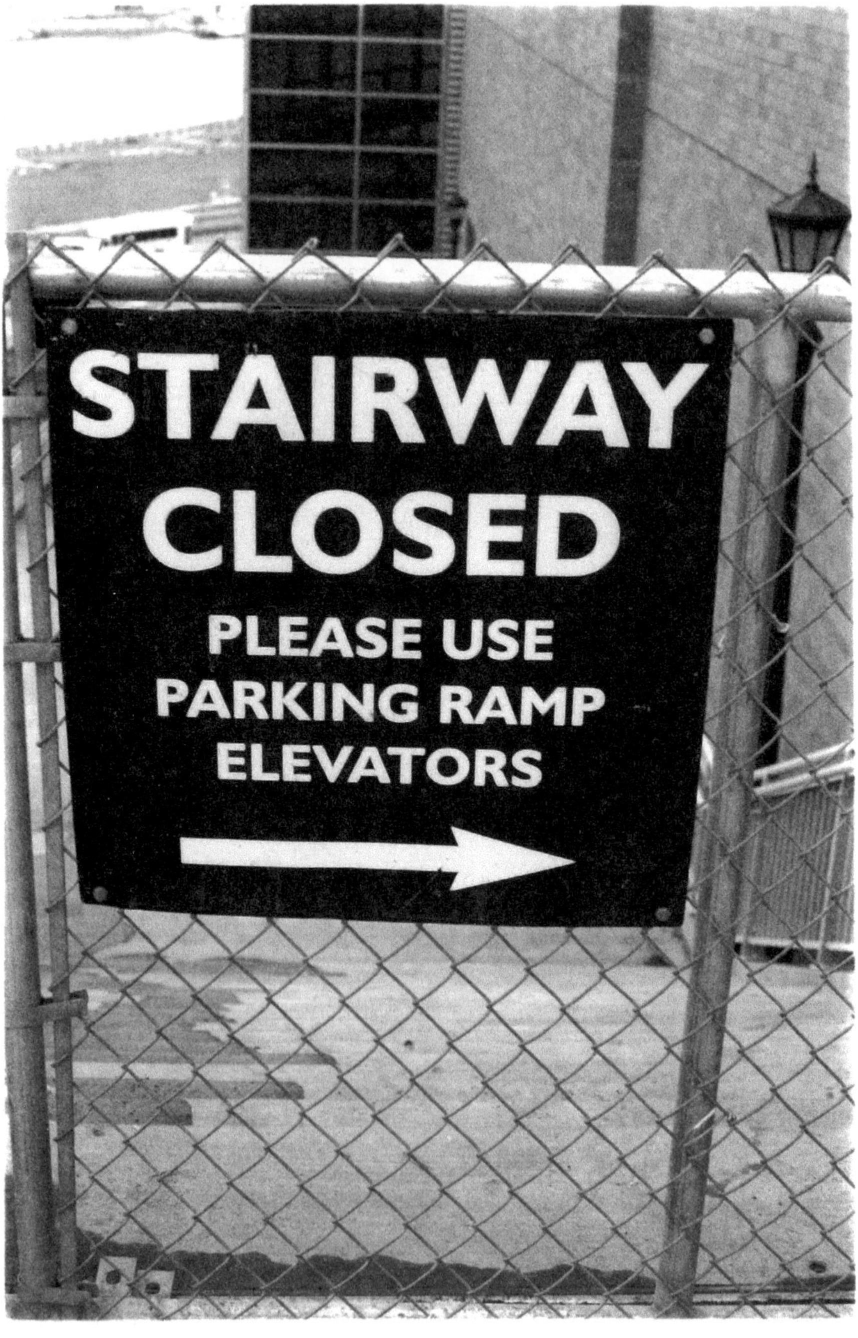
STAIRWAY
CLOSED
PLEASE USE
PARKING RAMP
ELEVATORS

Trapped

The light is trapped
Inside us by aching pain.
Our resentment
Festering, blistering
All hope with anger,
Keeping our light
Safe from the world
That destroyed our dreams.

We wait for courage
To nourish the love
We must find inside for
More than our own self.

We hope for faith that waters
The seeds of love
Sprouting from the
Jagged edges of
Our souls

For love that grows strong
Cracking through the
Mud we plastered over
Our hopeless offering

That one day love shines so
Brightly we can see
It reflected in every eye
And finally there is peace.

DENIAL   Date_____

Song: "You Can Love Yourself" Keb' Mo'

Observation: How do we stop inventing the downside?

Your Response: It makes me so angry . . . . .

ANGER   Date_____

Song: "Yesterday" Blues Beatles

Observation: How can you celebrate the new seasons of your life when resentment still fumes?

Your Response: Help me . . . . .

BROKEN HEART   Date_____

Song: "There Are Worse Things Than Being Alone"
Willie Nelson

Observation: A broken heart can show you just how insane the world is.

Your Response: Life is . . . . .

REMEMBERING   Date_____

Song: "Dance Me to the End of Love" Leonard Cohen

Observation: Real solutions come from God and not just from our own efforts.

Your Response: Time is . . . . .

ACCEPTANCE Date_____

Song: "The House of Love" Kelley Hunt

Observation: Our struggling for control can hide God's answers for our lives.

Your Response: God owes me . . . . .

MOVING ON Date_____

Song: "You've Got a Friend in Me" Randy Newman

Observation: Just like roses, the truth of your life has thorns.

Your Response: I don't care if . . . . .

DENIAL   Date_____

Song: "God Will Make a Way" Kathy Troccoli

Observation: Could the second choice for my life be okay for me? Would I let it be better than just okay?

Your Response: I will never . . . . .

ANGER   Date_____

Song: "Crooked" Amos Lee

Observation: How can God let life move this slowly? Where is the love in that?

Your Response: Will anyone ever . . . . .

BROKEN HEART   Date_____

Song: "Busy Being Blue" k.d. lang

Observation: Today is the first day of the rest of the life you don't want.

Your Response: I should have told you . . . . .

REMEMBERING   Date_____

Song: "For the Good Times" Al Green

Observation: I'm tired of chaos masquerading as the voice of God.

Your Response: I don't care if . . . . .

ACCEPTANCE   Date_____

Song: "I'll Remember You" Bob Dylan

Observation: What's in my heart is what I live with in my house.

Your Response: I did not know . . . . .

MOVING ON   Date_____

Song: "Feels Like Home" Diana Krall featuring Bryan Adams

Just what you wanted to hear: The light at the end of the tunnel is a train.

Your Response: The world is . . . . .

DENIAL Date_____

Song: "What's Forever For?" Michael Martin Murphey

Observation: Denial must not be allowed to run the world.

Your Response: I'm sorry . . . . .

ANGER Date_____

Song: "High Heel Sneakers" Ramsey Lewis

Observation: Fixating on what we have lost fuels our anger. The hard question is, what did we gain?

Your Response: Give me back . . . . .

BROKEN HEART Date_____

Song: "Red Wing" The Steel Wheels

Observation: Faith is the ability of setting aside your ego so God can work in your life.

Your Response: If only . . . . .

REMEMBERING Date_____

Song: "My Back Pages" Bob Dylan

Observation: I once had a belief in human love. Since you are gone, must I now believe in God?

Your Response: Show me . . . . .

ACCEPTANCE Date_____

Song: "Good Enough" Molly Tuttle

Observation: I want no more self-abuse about the past, the future, or the present.

Your Response: Help me . . . . .

MOVING ON Date_____

Song: "Amazing Grace" Diane Schuur

Observation: The only thing I own is my heart; it is also the only thing I can give away.

Your Response: I'm sorry . . . . .

DENIAL   Date_____

Song: "Sway" BoDeans

Observation: Living without faith is impossible. You just choose what to put your faith into.

Your Response: Give me back . . . . .

ANGER   Date_____

Song: "Things Go Wrong" Chris Isaak

Just what you wanted to hear: You may lose your mind, but you will find your soul.

Your Response: Why should I . . . . .

BROKEN HEART   Date_____

Song: "Save Yourself" KALEO

Observation: Hope is a weapon.

Your Response: Just tell me . . . . .

REMEMBERING   Date_____

Song: "Angel" Sarah McLachlan

Observation: Do we stop pretending about our lives when we are dead?

Your Response: Life owes me . . . . .

ACCEPTANCE   Date_____

Song: "Deep (Way Down)" Selah

Observation: Keep me from looking for love in all the wrong places.

Your Response: My days are so . . . . .

MOVING ON   Date_____

Song: "Lead Me Home" Jamey Johnson

Observation: Everything to be learned from life comes from feeling lost.

Your Response: Show me . . . . .

DENIAL   Date_____

Song: "Don't Fade Away" Amos Lee

Observation: Is it okay to hope to die soon?

Your Response: The truth . . . . .

ANGER   Date_____

Song: "This Year" The Mountain Goats

Observation: Faith in the unseen good is not meant to be easy.

Your Response: I want . . . . .

BROKEN HEART   Date_____

Song: "I Still Miss Someone" Martina McBride featuring Dolly Parton

Observation: The heart has dreams that never die.

Your Response: I should have told you . . . . .

REMEMBERING   Date_____

Song: "Halfway to Heaven" The Steel Wheels

Observation: Real love is endlessly reaching out to others, not afraid to spend everything.

Your Response: Will anyone ever . . . . .

ACCEPTANCE   Date_____

Song: "Leave the Light On" Chris Smither

Just what you wanted to hear: When did worry ever help?

Your Response: Help me . . . . .

MOVING ON   Date_____

Song: "Bless Us All" The Muppet Christmas Carol

Observation: Taking pleasure in what you do is the beginning of all healing.

Your Response: The heart won't . . . . .

"Welcome to Heaven's Gate. Our menu options have changed. Please listen carefully to the choices. If you know the extension number you may enter it at any time. Press 1 for Saint Peter, 2 for Saint Mary, 3 for Mohammed, 4 for Jesus, 5 for Buddha, 6 for Confucius, and 7 to return to the main menu."

Songs for Healing

Songs for Healing

Songs for Healing

Songs for Healing

Songs for Healing

Songs for Healing

Songs for Healing

Songs for Healing

Songs for Healing

Songs for Healing

Thank You

This journal is alive because of all my magical friends and family. Your smiles and tears are my most cherished memories.

And of course, thanks for the dedicated folks at Beaver's Pond Press, and my friend Kurt, who knew what to do when I didn't.